THE REVELS PLAYS

Former general editors
Clifford Leech
F. David Hoeniger
E. A. J. Honigmann
J. R. Mulryne
Eugene M. Waith

General editors
David Bevington, Richard Dutton, Alison Findlay,
Helen Ostovich and Martin White

THE MASSACRE AT PARIS

Manchester University Press

THE REVELS PLAYS

ANON *Thomas of Woodstock or King Richard the Second, Part One*
BEAUMONT *The Knight of the Burning Pestle*
BEAUMONT AND FLETCHER *A King and No King*
The Maid's Tragedy   Philaster, or Love Lies a-Bleeding
CHAPMAN *All Fools*
CHAPMAN *Bussy d'Ambois   An Humorous Day's Mirth*
CHAPMAN, JONSON, MARSTON *Eastward Ho*
DEKKER *The Shoemaker's Holiday*
DEKKER *Old Fortunatus*
FORD *Love's Sacrifice   The Lady's Trial*
HEYWOOD *The First and Second Parts of King Edward IV*
JONSON *The Alchemist   The Devil Is an Ass*
Epicene, or The Silent Woman   Every Man In His Humour
Every Man Out of His Humour   The Magnetic Lady
The New Inn   Poetaster   Sejanus: His Fall
The Staple of News   Volpone
LYLY *Campaspe* and *Sappho and Phao   Endymion*
Galatea and Midas   Love's Metamorphosis
Mother Bombie   The Woman in the Moon
MARLOWE *Doctor Faustus   Edward the Second*
The Jew of Malta   Tamburlaine the Great
MARSTON *Antonio and Mellida*
Antonio's Revenge   The Malcontent
MASSINGER *The Roman Actor*
MIDDLETON *A Game at Chess   Michaelmas Term*
A Trick to Catch the Old One
MIDDLETON AND DEKKER *The Roaring Girl*
MUNDAY AND OTHERS *Sir Thomas More*
PEELE *The Troublesome Reign of John, King of England*
David and Bathsheba
WEBSTER *The Duchess of Malfi*
WROTH *Love's Victory*

THE REVELS PLAYS

THE MASSACRE AT PARIS

CHRISTOPHER MARLOWE

edited by Mathew R. Martin

MANCHESTER
UNIVERSITY PRESS

Introduction, critical apparatus, etc.
© Mathew Martin 2021

The right of Mathew Martin to be identified as the editor of this work has been asserted by him in accordance with the Copyright, Designs and Patents Act 1988.

This edition published by Manchester University Press
Oxford Road, Manchester M13 9PL

www.manchesteruniversitypress.co.uk

British Library Cataloguing-in-Publication Data
A catalogue record for this book is available from the British Library

ISBN 978 1 5261 1775 5 hardback
ISBN 978 1 5261 1776 2 paperback

First published 2021
Paperback published 2025

The publisher has no responsibility for the persistence or accuracy of URLs for any external or third-party internet websites referred to in this book, and does not guarantee that any content on such websites is, or will remain, accurate or appropriate.

EU authorised representative for GPSR:
Easy Access System Europe – Mustamäe tee 50, 10621 Tallinn, Estonia, gpsr.requests@easproject.com

Typeset
by New Best-set Typesetters Ltd

Petal

Contents

GENERAL EDITORS' PREFACE	*page* viii
ACKNOWLEDGEMENTS	xi
LIST OF ABBREVIATIONS AND REFERENCES	xii
INTRODUCTION	1
The massacres at Paris, 1572	2
Sources and criticism	12
The Massacre at Paris, trauma, and memory	16
The Massacre at Paris and religious toleration	29
Performance history	39
The text	44
The Massacre at Paris	49
APPENDIX: THE COLLIER LEAF	137
INDEX	141

General Editors' Preface

Clifford Leech conceived of the Revels Plays as a series in the mid-1950s, modelling the project on the New Arden Shakespeare. The aim, as he wrote in 1958, was 'to apply to Shakespeare's predecessors, contemporaries, and successors the methods that are now used in Shakespeare's editing'. The plays chosen were to include well-known works from the early Tudor period to about 1700, as well as others less familiar but of literary and theatrical merit. 'The plays included', Leech wrote, 'should be such as to deserve and indeed demand performance'. We owe it to Clifford Leech that the idea became reality. He set the high standards of the series, ensuring that editors of individual volumes produced work of lasting merit, equally useful for teachers and students, theatre directors and actors. Clifford Leech remained General Editor until 1971, and was succeeded by F. David Hoeniger, who retired in 1985.

Ever since then, the Revels Plays have been under the direction of four or five general editors: initially David Bevington, E. A. J. Honigmann, J. R. Mulryne, and E. M. Waith. E. A. J. Honigmann retired in 2000 and was succeeded by Richard Dutton. E. M. Waith retired in 2003 and was succeeded by Alison Findlay and Helen Ostovich. J. R. Mulryne retired in 2010. Published originally by Methuen, the series is now published by the Manchester University Press, embodying essentially the same format, scholarly character, and high editorial standards of the series as first conceived. The series now concentrates on plays from the period 1558–1642. Some slight changes have been made: for example, starting in 1996 each index lists proper names and topics in the introduction and commentary, whereas earlier indexes focused only on words and phrases for which the commentary provided a gloss. Notes to the introduction are now placed together at the end, not at the foot of, the page. Collation and commentary notes continue, however, to appear on the relevant pages.

The introduction to each Revels play undertakes to offer, among other matters, a critical appraisal of the play's significant themes and images, its poetic and verbal fascinations, its historical context, its characteristics as a piece for the theatre, and its uses of the stage for which it was designed. Stage history is an important part of the story. In addition, the introduction presents as lucidly as possible the criteria for choice of copy-text and the editorial methods employed in presenting the play to a modern reader. The introduction also considers the play's date and, where relevant, its sources, together with its place in the work of the author and in the theatre of its time. If the play is by an author not previously represented in the series, a brief biography is provided.

The text of each Revels play, in accordance with established practice in the series, is edited afresh from the original text of best authority (in a few instances, texts), in modern spelling and punctuation and with speech headings that are consistent throughout. Elisions in the original are also silently regularised, except where metre would be affected by the change. Emendations, as distinguished from modernized spellings and punctuation, are introduced only in instances where error is patent or at least very probable, and where the corrected reading is persuasive. Act divisions are given only if they appear in the original, or if the structure of the play clearly points to them. Those act and scene divisions not in the original are provided in small type. Square brackets are also used for any other additions to, or changes in, the stage directions of the original.

Rather than provide a comprehensive and historical variorum collation, Revels Plays editions focus on those variants which require the critical attention of serious textual students. All departures of substance from the copy-text are listed, including any significant relineation and those changes in punctuation which involve to any degree a decision between alternative interpretations. The collation notes do not include such accidentals as turned letters or changes in the font. Additions to stage directions are not noted in the collations, since those additions are already made clear by the use of brackets. On the other hand, press corrections in the copy-text are duly collated, as based on a careful consultation of as many copies of the original edition or editions as are needed to ensure that the printing history of those originals is accurately reported. Of later emendations of the text by subsequent editors, only those are reported which still deserve attention as alternative readings.

One of the hallmarks of the Revels Plays is the thoroughness of their annotations. Besides explaining the meanings of difficult words and passages, the annotations provide commentary on customs or usage, on the text, on stage business – indeed, on anything that can be pertinent and helpful. On occasion, when long notes are required and are too lengthy to fit comfortably at the foot of the page below the text, they are printed at the end of the complete text.

Appendices are used to present any commendatory poems on the dramatist and play in question, documents about the play's reception and contemporary history, classical sources, casting analyses, music, and any other relevant material.

Each volume contains an index to the commentary, in which particular attention is drawn to meanings for words not listed in the OED, and (starting in 1996, as indicated above) an indexing of proper names and topics in the introduction and commentary.

Our hope is that plays edited in this fashion will promote further scholarly and theatrical investigation of one of the richest periods in theatrical history.

DAVID BEVINGTON
RICHARD DUTTON
ALISON FINDLAY
HELEN OSTOVICH
MARTIN WHITE

Acknowledgements

My thanks go to the staff at the libraries that house copies of the octavo of *The Massacre at Paris* for facilitating the digital reproduction of those copies. Brock University's Humanities Research Institute provided funds to defray the cost of the digital reproductions. Thanks also to Taylor and Francis for permission to reproduce in adapted form material from my book, *Tragedy and Trauma in the Plays of Christopher Marlowe* (2015), and to Helen Ostovich for permission to reproduce in adapted form material from a seminar paper posted on the *Three Ladies of London* conference (2015) website.

Abbreviations and References

EARLY EDITION OF *THE MASSACRE AT PARIS*

O	Christopher Marlowe, *The Massacre at Paris: With the Death of the Duke of Guise* (London: Edward White, n.d.)
OBL	Copy of O at the British Library, London
OBod	Copy of O at the Bodleian Library, Oxford
OCh	Copy of O at the Chapin Library, Williams College, Massachusetts
OFo	Copy of O at the Folger Shakespeare Library, Washington, DC
OHu	Copy of O at the Huntington Library, San Marino, CA
OLC	Copy of O at the Library of Congress, Washington, DC
OMa	Copy of O at the Pepys Library, Magdalene College, Cambridge
ONe	Copy of O at the Newberry Library, Chicago, IL
OPa	Copy of O at the Parker Library, Corpus Christi College, Cambridge
OVAM	Copy of O at the Victoria and Albert Museum, Dyce Collection, London

MODERN EDITIONS OF *THE MASSACRE AT PARIS*

Bennett	*The Jew of Malta* and *The Massacre at Paris*, ed. H. S. Bennett, 1931 (New York: Gordian Press, 1966)
Brooke	*The Massacre at Paris*, in *The Works of Christopher Marlowe*, ed. C. F. Tucker Brooke (Oxford: Clarendon Press, 1910)
Broughton	*The Massacre at Paris*, ed. James Broughton (London: Chappell, 1818)
Bullen	*The Massacre at Paris*, in vol. 2 of *The Works of Christopher Marlowe*, ed. A. H. Bullen, 3 vols (London: John Nimmo, 1885)
Dyce	*The Massacre at Paris*, in vol. 2 of *The Works of Christopher Marlowe*, ed. Alexander Dyce, 3 vols (London: William Pickering, 1850)

Dyce 2	*The Massacre at Paris*, in vol. 2 of *The Works of Christopher Marlowe*, ed. Alexander Dyce, 3 vols (London: William Pickering, 1858)
Esche	*The Massacre at Paris*, ed. Edward J. Esche, in vol. 5 of *The Complete Works of Christopher Marlowe*, 5 vols (Oxford: Clarendon Press, 1998)
Greg	*The Massacre at Paris*, ed. W. W. Greg (Oxford: Malone Society Reprints, 1929 [1928])
Malone	Marginal note by Edmund Malone in OBod
Oliver	*Dido Queen of Carthage* and *The Massacre at Paris*, ed. H. J. Oliver (Cambridge, MA: Harvard University Press, 1968)
Ribner	*The Complete Plays of Christopher Marlowe*, ed. Irving Ribner (New York: Odyssey Press, 1963)
Robinson	*The Massacre at Paris*, in vol. 2 of *The Works of Christopher Marlowe*, ed. G. Robinson, 3 vols (London: Pickering, 1826)

OTHER REFERENCES

Abraham and Torok	Nicholas Abraham and Maria Torok, 'The Topography of Reality: Sketching a Metapsychology of Secrets', in *The Shell and the Kernel*, ed. and trans. Nicholas T. Rand (Chicago: University of Chicago Press, 1994), 157–61
Allott	Robert Allott, ed., *England's Parnassus* (London: N.L.C.B and T.H., 1600)
'The answer'	'The answer of her Majesty to the aforesaid letters of the Great Turk', in *The Jew of Malta*, by Christopher Marlowe, ed. Mathew R. Martin (Peterborough, ON: Broadview Press, 2012), 240–3
Arden of Faversham	*The Tragedy of Master Arden of Faversham*, ed. Martin White (London: Ernest Benn, 1982)
Ardolino	Frank Ardolino, 'Contention within a Little Room: Marlowe, Kyd, the Dutch Church Libel, and the Paris Massacre', *Journal of Evolutionary Psychology* 16.3–4 (1995), 242–7

Bacon	Francis Bacon, 'Of Revenge', in *The Major Works*, ed. Brian Vickers (Oxford: Oxford University Press, 1996), 347–8
Baldo	Jonathan Baldo, 'Wars of Memory in *Henry V*', *Shakespeare Quarterly* 47.2 (1996), 132–59
Beaumont	Francis Beaumont, *The Knight of the Burning Pestle*, ed. Michael Hattaway (London: A. and C. Black, 1986)
Bevington	David Bevington, *Tudor Drama and Politics: A Critical Approach to Topical Meaning* (Cambridge, MA: Harvard University Press, 1968)
Bodin	Jean Bodin, *The Six Books of a Commonweal*, trans. Richard Knolles (London, 1606)
Bowers	Rick Bowers, '*The Massacre at Paris*: Marlowe's Messy Consensus Narrative', in *Marlowe, History, and Sexuality: New Critical Essays on Christopher Marlowe*, ed. Paul Whitfield White (New York: AMS, 1998), 131–41
Brennan	Mary Brennan, review of 1981 Glasgow Citizens' Theatre production of *The Massacre at Paris*, *The Glasgow Herald*, 2 February 1981
Briggs	Julia Briggs, 'Marlowe's *Massacre at Paris*: A Reconsideration', *Review of English Studies* 34 (1983), 257–78
Caesar	Caius Julius Caesar, *Gallic War*, ed. James B. Greenough (New York: Ginn, 1898)
Cahill	Patricia Cahill, 'The Feel of the Slaughterhouse: Affective Temporalities and Marlowe's *The Massacre at Paris*', in *Affect Theory and Early Modern Texts: Politics, Ecologies, and Form*, ed. Amanda Bailey and Mario DiGangi (Basingstoke: Palgrave Macmillan, 2017), 155–74
Carroll	Stuart Carroll, *Martyrs and Murderers: The Guise Family and the Making of Europe* (Oxford: Oxford University Press, 2009)
Caruth	Cathy Caruth, *Unclaimed Experience: Trauma, Narrative, and History* (Baltimore, MD: Johns Hopkins University Press, 1996)

Colynet	Antony Colynet, *The True History of the Civil Wars of France* (London, 1591)
Coveney	Michael Coveney, review of 1981 Glasgow Citizens' Theatre production of *The Massacre at Paris*, *The Financial Times*, 2 February 1981
Cummings	Brian Cummings, '"Dead March": Liturgy and Mimesis in Shakespeare's Funerals', *Shakespeare* 8.4 (2012), 368–85
Davis	Natalie Zemon Davis, 'The Rites of Violence: Religious Riot in Sixteenth-Century France', *Past and Present* 59 (May 1973), 51–91
Deats	Sara Munson Deats, '*Dido, Queen of Carthage* and *The Massacre at Paris*', in *The Cambridge Companion to Christopher Marlowe*, ed. Patrick Cheney (Cambridge: Cambridge University Press, 2004), 193–206
Dent	R. W. Dent, *Proverbial Language in English Drama Exclusive of Shakespeare, 1495–1616* (Berkeley, CA: University of California Press, 1984)
Dessen and Thomson	Alan C. Dessen and Leslie Thomson, *A Dictionary of Stage Directions in English Drama, 1580–1642* (Cambridge: Cambridge University Press, 1999)
Doctor Faustus	Christopher Marlowe, *Doctor Faustus: The B Text*, ed. Mathew R. Martin (Peterborough, ON: Broadview Press, 2013)
Drummond	William Drummond, 'Letter (f), from William Drummond of Hawthornden', in vol. 5 of *The Works of Ben Jonson*, ed. David Bevington, Martin Butler, and Ian Donaldson, 7 vols (Cambridge: Cambridge University Press, 2012), 395–8
Dubec-Crespin	Jean Dubec-Crespin, *The History of the Great Emperor Tamerlan*, in Christopher Marlowe, *Tamburlaine the Great Part One and Part Two*, ed. Mathew R. Martin (Peterborough, ON: Broadview Press, 2014)
Edward II	Christopher Marlowe, *Edward the Second*, ed. Mathew R. Martin (Peterborough, ON: Broadview Press, 2010)

Eriksen	Roy T. Eriksen, 'Construction in Marlowe's *Massacre at Paris*', in *Papers from the First Nordic Conference for English Studies*, ed. S. Johansson and B. Tysdahl (Oslo: Institute of English Studies, 1981), 41–54
Estate	Anon., *The Estate of English Fugitives under the King of Spain and His Ministers* (London: John Drawater, 1595)
Farmer	David Hugh Farmer, *The Oxford Dictionary of Saints*, 2nd edn (Oxford: Oxford University Press, 1987)
First Part of the Contention	Anon., *The First Part of the Contention of the Two Famous Houses of York and Lancaster, with the Death of the Good Duke Humphrey* (London: Thomas Creed, 1594)
Foakes	R. A. Foakes, ed., *Henslowe's Diary*, 2nd edn (Cambridge: Cambridge University Press, 2002)
Forker	Charles R. Forker, ed., *Edward the Second*, by Christopher Marlowe (Manchester: Manchester University Press, 1994)
Foxe	John Foxe, *Acts and Monuments*, 1563 (New York: AMS Press, 1965)
Frisch	Andrea Frisch, *Forgetting Differences: Tragedy, Historiography, and the French Wars of Religion* (Edinburgh: Edinburgh University Press, 2015)
Garrisson, *Guerre civile*	Janine Garrisson, *Guerre civile et compromis* (Paris: Éditions du Seuil, 1991)
Garrisson, *La Saint-Barthélemy*	Janine Garrisson, *1572, La Saint-Barthélemy* (Brussels: Éditions Complexe, 2000)
Godshalk	W. L. Godshalk, *The Marlovian World Picture* (The Hague: Mouton, 1974)
Goffman	Daniel Goffman, *The Ottoman Empire and Early Modern Europe* (Cambridge: Cambridge University Press, 2002)
Golding	'The Edict or proclamation set forth by the French King upon the pacifying of the troubles in France ... Read and published in the presence of the said King, sitting in his parliament, the xiiii day of May, 1576', trans. Arthur Golding (London, 1576)

Greene	Robert Greene, *The Tragedy of Selimus Emperor of the Turks*, ed. Mathew R. Martin (Peterborough, ON: Broadview Press, forthcoming 2021)
Greenfield and Gurr	John Greenfield and Andrew Gurr, 'The Rose Theatre, London: The State of Knowledge and What We Still Need to Know', *Antiquity* 78 (June 2004), 330–40
Grimal	Pierre Grimal, *The Dictionary of Classical Mythology*, trans. A. R. Maxwell-Hyslop (Oxford: Blackwell, 1996)
Gurr, *Shakespearean Stage*	Andrew Gurr, *The Shakespearean Stage 1574–1642*, 3rd edn (Cambridge: Cambridge University Press, 2001)
Gurr, *Shakespeare's Opposites*	Andrew Gurr, *Shakespeare's Opposites: The Admiral's Company 1594–1625* (Cambridge: Cambridge University Press, 2009)
Guy	John Guy, *Tudor England* (Oxford: Oxford University Press, 1988)
Hailey	R. Carter Hailey, 'The Publication Date of Marlowe's *Massacre at Paris*, with a Note on the Collier Leaf', *Marlowe Studies: An Annual* 1 (2011), 25–40
Hillman	Richard Hillman, *Shakespeare, Marlowe and the Politics of France* (Basingstoke: Palgrave, 2002)
Holt	Mack P. Holt, *The French Wars of Religion, 1562–1629*, 2nd edn (Cambridge: Cambridge University Press, 2005)
Homily	*An Homilie Agaynst Disobedience and Wylful Rebellion* (London, 1570)
Honan	Park Honan, *Christopher Marlowe: Poet and Spy* (Oxford: Oxford University Press, 2005)
Hotman, *Life*	François Hotman, *The Life of the Most Godly, Valiant and Noble ... Jasper Coligny*, trans. Arthur Golding (London, 1576)
Hotman, *True and Plain Report*	François Hotman [Ernest Varamund], *A True and Plain Report of the Furious Outrages of France* (London [Striveling, Scotland], 1573)
Hurault	Michel Hurault, *An Excellent Discourse Upon the Now Present Estate of France*, trans. E. A. (London, 1592)

Ichikawa	Mariko Ichikawa, *The Shakespearean Stage Space* (Cambridge: Cambridge University Press, 2013)
Imber	Colin Imber, *The Ottoman Empire*, 2nd edn (New York: Palgrave Macmillan, 2009)
Jew of Malta	Christopher Marlowe, *The Jew of Malta*, ed. Mathew R. Martin (Peterborough, ON: Broadview Press, 2012)
Jordan	W. K. Jordan, *The Development of Religious Toleration in England* (Gloucester, MA: Peter Smith, 1965)
Jouanna	Arlette Jouanna, *The St Bartholomew's Day Massacre*, trans. Joseph Bergin (Manchester: Manchester University Press, 2013)
Kaplan	Benjamin J. Kaplan, *Divided By Faith: Religious Conflict and the Practice of Toleration* (Cambridge, MA: Harvard University Press, 2007)
Kingdon	Robert M. Kingdon, *Myths about the St. Bartholomew Day Massacres 1572–1576* (Cambridge, MA: Harvard University Press, 1988)
Kirk	Andrew Kirk, 'Marlowe and the Disordered Face of French History', *Studies in English Literature 1500–1900* 35.2 (1995), 193–213
Knight	Sarah Knight, 'Flat Dichotomists and Learned Men: Ramism in Elizabethan Drama and Satire', in *Ramus, Pedagogy and the Liberal Arts*, ed. Steven J. Reid and Emma Annette Wilson (Burlington, VT: Ashgate, 2011), 47–67
Kocher, 'Contemporary Pamphlet Backgrounds'	Paul Kocher, 'Contemporary Pamphlet Backgrounds for Marlowe's *The Massacre at Paris*', *Modern Language Quarterly* 8.2 (1947), 151–73
Kocher, 'Contemporary Pamphlet Backgrounds Part Two'	Paul Kocher, 'Contemporary Pamphlet Backgrounds for Marlowe's *The Massacre at Paris*. Part Two', *Modern Language Quarterly* 8.3 (1947), 309–18
Kocher, 'François Hotman'	'François Hotman and Marlowe's *The Massacre at Paris*', *PMLA* 56.2 (1941), 349–68

Kyd, *Cornelia*	Thomas Kyd, *Cornelia* (London, 1594)
Kyd, *ST*	Thomas Kyd, *The Spanish Tragedy*, ed. J. R. Mulryne (London: A. and C. Black, 1989)
LaCapra	Dominick LaCapra, *Writing History, Writing Trauma* (Baltimore, MD: Johns Hopkins University Press, 2001)
Lecler	Joseph Lecler, *Toleration and the Reformation*, trans. T. L. Westow, 2 vols (New York: Association Press, 1960)
Lee	Nathaniel Lee, *The Massacre of Paris*, in vol. 2 of *The Works of Nathaniel Lee*, ed. Thomas B. Stroup and Arthur L. Cooke (Metuchen, NJ: Scarecrow, 1968)
Levin	Harry Levin, *The Overreacher: A Study of Christopher Marlowe*. (Cambridge, MA: Harvard University Press, 1952)
MacKenzie	Clayton MacKenzie, *Deathly Experiments: A Study of Icons and Emblems of Mortality in Christopher Marlowe's Plays* (New York: AMS Press, 2010)
Maguire	Laurie Maguire, *Shakespearean Suspect Texts: The 'Bad' Quartos and their Contexts* (Cambridge: Cambridge University Press, 1996)
Manley and MacLean	Lawrence Manley and Sally-Beth MacLean, *Lord Strange's Men and Their Plays* (New Haven, CT: Yale University Press, 2014)
McKinnon	Catriona McKinnon, *Toleration: A Critical Introduction* (New York: Routledge, 2006)
Memoirs	Margaret de Valois, *Secret and Historic Memoirs of the Courts of France* (Philadelphia: Rittenhouse Press, n.d.)
Neale	J. E. Neale, *Queen Elizabeth I* (Harmondsworth: Penguin, 1960)
Nederman	Cary J. Nederman, *Worlds of Difference: European Discourses of Toleration c. 1100–c.1550* (University Park, PA: Pennsylvania State University Press, 2000)
Nicholl	Charles Nicholl, *The Reckoning: The Murder of Christopher Marlowe* (London: Picador, 1992)

OED	*Oxford English Dictionary Online* (Oxford: Oxford University Press, 2013), http://www.oed.com
Oliver, review	Cordelia Oliver, review of 1981 Glasgow Citizens' Theatre production of *The Massacre at Paris*, *The Guardian*, 3 February 1981
Orman	Steve Robert Orman, '*The Massacre at Paris*, presented by The Dolphin Back at the Rose Playhouse, Bankside, October 2014', *Early Modern Literary Studies* 18.1–2 (2015), 1–4
Ovid	*Metamorphoses*, trans. Arthur Golding, 1567, ed. John Frederick Nims (Philadelphia: Paul Dry Books, 2000)
Parker	John Parker, 'Barabas and Charles I', in *Placing the Plays of Christopher Marlowe: Fresh Cultural Contexts*, ed. Sara Munson Deats and Robert A. Logan (Aldershot: Ashgate, 2008), 167–81
Peele	George Peele, *David and Bathsheba*, ed. Mathew R. Martin (Manchester: Manchester University Press, 2018)
Perry	Curtis Perry, 'The Politics of Access and Representations of the Sodomite King in Early Modern England', *Renaissance Quarterly* 53.4 (2000), 1054–83
Pey	Serge Pey, review of *Massacre at Paris* presented by Théâtre 2 l'Acte at the Théâtre du Ring in November 2016, in *1572, Massacre à Paris: Revue de presse* (Théâtre du Ring, 2016), 4
Pitts	Vincent J. Pitts, *Henry IV of France: His Reign and Age* (Baltimore, MD: Johns Hopkins University Press, 2009)
Plowden	Alison Plowden, *Elizabeth I* (London: Sutton, 2004)
Poirier	Michel Poirier, *Christopher Marlowe* (London: Chatto and Windus, 1968)
Poole	Kristen Poole, 'Garbled Martyrdom in Christopher Marlowe's *The Massacre at Paris*', *Comparative Drama* 32.1 (1998), 1–25

Potter	David Potter, 'Marlowe's *Massacre at Paris* and the Reputation of Henri III of France', in *Christopher Marlowe and English Renaissance Culture*, ed. Darryl Grantley and Peter Roberts (Aldershot: Scolar Press, 1996), 70–95
Ramus	Petrus Ramus, *The Logic of the Most Excellent Philosopher P. Ramus Martyr*, trans. Roland MacIlmaine (London, 1574)
Riggs	David Riggs, *The World of Christopher Marlowe* (New York: Henry Holt, 2004)
Rivere de Carles	Natalie Rivere de Carles, review of *The Massacre at Paris*, presented by Compagnie X ici at Théâtre National de Toulouse in March 2007, *Shakespeare Bulletin* 25.4 (2007), 143–7
Roberts	Penny Roberts, 'Marlowe's *The Massacre at Paris*: A Historical Perspective', *Renaissance Studies* 9.4 (1995), 430–41
Robson	W. W. Robson, review of 1981 Glasgow Citizens' Theatre production of *The Massacre at Paris*, *Times Literary Supplement*, 13 February 1981
Rothberg	Michael Rothberg, *Traumatic Realism: The Demands of Holocaust Representation* (Minneapolis, MN: University of Minnesota Press, 2000)
Sanders	Wilbur Sanders, *The Dramatist and the Received Idea* (Cambridge: Cambridge University Press, 1968)
Scanlon	Thomas Scanlon, *The Difficulty of Tolerance: Essays in Political Philosophy* (Cambridge: Cambridge University Press, 2003)
Schmitt and Skinner	Charles B. Schmitt and Quentin Skinner, eds, *The Cambridge History of Renaissance Philosophy* (Cambridge: Cambridge University Press, 1988)
Serres, *Fourth Part of Commentaries*	Jean Serres, *The Fourth Part of Commentaries of the Civil Wars in France*, trans. Thomas Tymme (London, 1576)
Serres, *General Inventorie*	Jean Serres, *A General Inventorie of the History of France*, trans. Edward Grimeston (London, 1607)

Seward	Desmond Seward, *The First Bourbon* (Boston: Gambit, 1971)
Shakespeare	William Shakespeare, *The Complete Works of Shakespeare*, ed. David Bevington, 7th edn (New York: Longman, 2004)
Skinner	Quentin Skinner, *The Foundations of Modern Political Thought*, 2 vols (Cambridge: Cambridge University Press, 1978)
Solnon	Jean François Solnon, *Henri III* (Paris: Perrin, 2007)
Steane	J. B. Steane, *Marlowe: A Critical Study* (Cambridge: Cambridge University Press, 1964)
Stubbes	John Stubbes, *The Discovery of a Gaping Gulf* (London, 1579)
Tamburlaine	Christopher Marlowe, *Tamburlaine the Great Part One and Part Two*, ed. Mathew R. Martin (Peterborough, ON: Broadview Press, 2014)
Thomas and Tydeman	Vivien Thomas and William Tydeman, eds, *Christopher Marlowe: The Plays and their Sources* (London: Routledge, 1994)
Thomson, 'Beds'	Leslie Thomson, 'Beds on the Early Modern Stage', *Early Theatre* 19.2 (2016), 31–57
Thomson, 'Staging'	Leslie Thomson, 'Marlowe's Staging of Meaning', *Medieval and Renaissance Drama in England* 18 (2005), 19–36
Tilley	M. P. Tilley, *A Dictionary of Proverbs in England in the Sixteenth and Seventeenth Centuries* (Ann Arbor, MI: University of Michigan Press, 1950)
Tribble	Evelyn Tribble, '"Then breathe awhile": Compression, Kinesis, and Temporality in *The Massacre at Paris*', in *Christopher Marlowe, Theatrical Commerce, and the Book Trade*, ed. Kirk Melnikoff and Roslyn L. Knutson (Cambridge: Cambridge University Press, 2018), 56–67
True Tragedy	Anon., *The True Tragedy of Richard Duke of York* (London: Thomas Millington, 1595)
Vindiciae	*Vindiciae contra Tyrannos, a Defence of Liberty against Tyrants* (London, 1648)

Walsh	Brian Walsh, *Unsettled Toleration: Religious Difference on the Shakespearean Stage* (Oxford: Oxford University Press, 2016)
Walsham	Alexandra Walsham, *Charitable Hatred: Tolerance and Intolerance in England, 1500–1700* (Manchester: Manchester University Press, 2006)
Whetstone	George Whetstone, *The English Mirror* (London, 1586)
Wiggins	Martin Wiggins, 'Marlowe's Chronology and Canon', in *Christopher Marlowe in Context*, ed. Emily C. Bartels and Emma Smith (Cambridge: Cambridge University Press, 2013), 7–14

Introduction

On 30 May 1593 Ingram Frizer fatally stabbed Christopher Marlowe through the eye in an inn in Deptford. Some biographers have suggested that the killing was an assassination and Marlowe the 'victim ... of the court intrigues that flourished' (Nicholl, 329) in *fin-de-siècle* Elizabethan England, although who might have given the orders for the hit remains unclear. Four years earlier, on 1 August 1589, the monk Jacques Clément fatally stabbed one of the major characters of Marlowe's *The Massacre at Paris*, Henry III, in the stomach with a poisoned knife at the French monarch's villa just outside Paris. This most certainly was an assassination, although even modern historians are uncertain about who was implicated. Both men died young: born on 23 February 1564, Marlowe was 29 when death in the guise of a minor Elizabethan intelligence agent overtook him; Henry III met his cowled fate at the age of 38. As young as they were, though, both had already achieved considerable notoriety, Marlowe as an atheistic and homosexual London dramatist, and Henry as a blasphemous and homosexual French king. These eerie parallels, of course, belie the worlds of difference separating the playwright from his character. Henry was the son of Henry II and Catherine de Medici; Marlowe was the son of John and Katherine Marlowe, a Canterbury shoemaker and his wife. Henry's childhood and youth were characterised by all the privilege one would expect a member of the French royal family to enjoy, while Marlowe's might best be described in terms of the schools he attended as a poor boy on scholarship: his grammar school was King's School in Canterbury, after which he attended Corpus Christi College at Cambridge on a Parker scholarship, commencing in 1580 and receiving his BA and MA in 1584 and 1587 respectively.

Even before completing his MA, Marlowe seems to have led a double life as a low-level agent in the Elizabethan intelligence service and playwright for the London professional theatres. The former may have taken him to Paris in 1584–85 as a courier (Honan, 147), and it was rumoured to have taken him as a double agent to the English Catholic seminary at Reims, a rumour that the Privy Council had to quash in order for Marlowe to be awarded his MA (Honan,

153–4). The latter, his play writing, took him to London's many inn, hall, and open-air theatre venues. Marlowe may have written his first play during his Cambridge days: *Dido Queen of Carthage* has typically been dated to this period, and its title page states that it was performed by the Children of Her Majesty's Chapel, a boy company performing in an indoor theatre in the London liberty of Blackfriars. As his exploits in the Low Countries counterfeiting money in 1592 demonstrate (Riggs, 274–5), Marlowe's career in the secret service did not halt upon his graduation. Nor did his career as a dramatist. Before his untimely end Marlowe wrote six plays for the adult companies performing on the stages of London's open-air playhouses: *1* and *2 Tamburlaine* (1587–88), *Doctor Faustus* (1589), *The Jew of Malta* (1589–92), *Edward II* (1592–93), and *The Massacre at Paris* (1592–93). The dates given here are not uncontested (see Wiggins, 'Marlowe's Chronology and Canon', for a recent account of the issues), but regardless of their exact order, the plays testify to an outburst of intense creative activity over a short span of time. Before his death Marlowe also produced significant non-dramatic poetry, such as his trend-setting epyllion 'Hero and Leander' and his popular 'Passionate Shepherd to His Love', and translations of Ovid's erotic *Elegies* and Lucan's *Pharsalia*, a rendition in epic form of the civil war between Julius Caesar and Pompey.

Though critics have tried, it is difficult to perceive a developmental trajectory in Marlowe's dramatic oeuvre. This is perhaps the result of the uncertain dating of the plays, and it is also the case that Marlowe's plays return repeatedly to the same general concerns, such as weak monarchs or the Machiavellian pursuit of power, although approaching these concerns in different ways. Connections between *The Massacre at Paris* and Marlowe's other plays will be made throughout this introduction to illustrate this consistency. Nonetheless, when compared to the rhetorically scintillating *Tamburlaine* plays, *The Massacre at Paris*, often dismissed as Marlowe's worst play, suggests development as well as repetition. In what may be his last play, Marlowe presents his most brutally unsentimental critique of religiously inspired violence.

THE MASSACRES AT PARIS, 1572

The Massacre at Paris's tragic action begins with a festive event: the royal wedding of Henry of Navarre and Margaret Valois in Paris at the end of August in 1572. It was a grand occasion, as was befitting both the royal stature of the bride and groom and the larger political hopes that many in France placed on the marriage to put an end to the civil and religious strife that had been tearing France apart since 1562, when François, Duke of Guise had triggered the first French War of Religion by massacring a group of worshipping Huguenots in the small French town of Vassy (Holt, 48). The groom was Henry Bourbon, King of Navarre, a small, semi-independent kingdom bordering on Spain just north of the Pyrenees. The bride, Margaret, was a princess, the daughter of Catherine de Medici and the deceased French monarch Henry II. Her brother, Charles IX, had worn the French crown since 1560. The match made excellent sense dynastically, and both Catherine de Medici and Jeanne d'Albret, Henry's mother, had negotiated hard to make it happen. As senior male of the Bourbon lineage, Henry was next in line to the French throne after Margaret's brothers Charles, Henry (Duke of Anjou when the play begins, and Henry III after Charles's death), and François (Duke d'Alençon). By uniting the two royal families of Bourbon and Valois, the marriage had the potential to diminish if not entirely eliminate the age-old problem of the sapping of centralised monarchical authority through destructive dynastic competition.

Equally significant were the religious implications of the marriage. Henry was a Protestant and, along with the Prince of Condé and Gaspar Coligny, the Lord Admiral, he was the leader of the Huguenots (as the French Protestants were known) in the internal religious wars that had overtaken France. Margaret was a Catholic, and the hope was that the marriage might further the acceptance of Huguenot Protestantism in France or (on the Catholic side) that Margaret's influence might lead eventually to Henry's conversion to Catholicism. Not all Catholics, or Huguenots, were happy with the religious mixing entailed by the union, however. In the play's first scene Catherine menacingly warns Navarre that 'our difference in religion / Might be a means to cross you in your love' (15-16). Historically Catherine was one of the major champions of the marriage, but here Marlowe uses her to voice a sentiment shared by many on both sides of the confessional divide, including the Pope, who refused to issue the papal dispensation necessary to validate the wedding ceremony (Jouanna, 64). In the event, Henry did convert to Catholicism in 1593 in order to be crowned as Henry IV in Paris in 1594 ('Paris is worth a Mass', he is reported to have quipped); his conversion allowed him to persuade the Pope to grant him a divorce from Margaret in 1599 and marry Marie de Medici a year later.

The exchange among Charles, Navarre, and Catherine with which the first scene of the play commences is shaped by the dynastic and religious hopes weighing on the marriage and by an uneasy recognition of the sizeable impediments to those hopes. '[L]et that rest' (17), Charles responds to his mother's ominous remark to Navarre, but the play does not, quickly bringing forward yet another major obstacle to the marriage's success: the House of Guise and its chief representative, Henry, Duke of Guise. The Guise had close familial connections with both the Bourbon and Valois royal families. Mary Queen of Scots, who was Queen of France during the brief reign of her husband François II (r. 1559–60), Charles IX's older brother, belonged to the Guise clan. At the age of seven, Henry attended Navarre College, where two of his schoolmates were the young Henry of Navarre and Henry, Duke of Anjou (Carroll, 185). Later, Henry and Margaret had a love affair several years before Margaret's marriage to Navarre (Carroll, 188–9). (Charles and Anjou put a stop to the affair, which is the focus of Nathaniel Lee's play *Massacre at Paris* [1690].) The Guise had proven themselves loyal to the crown in the past and during François II's reign had exercised considerable influence, yet they were ambitious, staunchly Catholic, had ties with ultra-Catholic and imperialist Spain, and had deeply personal as well as political reasons to be hostile to the Huguenots: in 1563, during the first War of Religion, Henry's father François was assassinated at the siege of Orléans at the instigation, it was generally believed, of Lord Admiral Coligny, whose influence at court over Charles had been growing from 1570 precisely because of his opposition to Spanish imperialism in Europe.

Marlowe's play omits or merely glances at many of the finer points of this complex situation. No reference is made to the love affair, for example, or to revenge for his father's death as one of Guise's motivations for the assassination of the Admiral. Nonetheless, the play preserves the situation's broad outlines. Even before he makes his first appearance on stage, Guise is represented as an alienated but dangerous figure, hostile to the French Protestant cause in general and the royal marriage in particular. Remaining with the other Huguenots outside the church after Margaret and others have gone in to celebrate the Mass, Navarre chortles that 'Now Guise may storm but do us little hurt, / Having the King, Queen Mother on our sides / To stop the malice of his envious heart'

(27–9). His sense of security soon evaporates, however, as Guise's murderous intentions, Spanish and papal connections, and dynastic ambitions are recalled. Not surprisingly, the scene concludes with Navarre's exhortation to his companions to 'go to the church and pray' (54). The scene immediately following only confirms these impressions. 'If ever Hymen loured at marriage rites, / And had his altars decked with dusky lights' (2.1–2), announces Guise upon entering, 'This day, this hour, this fatal night / Shall show the fury of them all' (7–8). Guise then arranges for the assassination of Navarre's mother and the Admiral, urges himself to 'deal thyself a king' (89), and declares that 'The plot is laid, and things shall come to pass / Where resolution strives for victory' (106–7).

The assassinations of the Queen of Navarre and the Admiral constitute only the prologue of the plot to which Guise is referring, of course. His plot's main action is the main action of the first half of the play: the St Bartholomew's Day massacres, which took place on 24–30 August in Paris and then extended into other provincial French cities. For purposes of dramatic condensation and intensification, Marlowe has tampered with the historical facts in some significant ways. Navarre's mother, for example, died on 9 June, before the wedding, and Guise was not involved in her death. Marlowe brings her death forward to accompany the assassination attempt on the Admiral in order to double Guise's villainy and establish his centrality in the unfolding of the subsequent terrors. Guise almost certainly was the moving force behind the assassination attempt on the Admiral on 22 August. The man who pulled the trigger, Charles de Louviers, seigneur de Maurevet, was a Guise client, and Guise later endowed him with a substantial pension (Jouanna, 74–5). The assassination attempt was the event that sparked the massacres that followed. When he was shot, the Admiral was returning from a royal council meeting at which he had been presenting various Huguenot complaints. In such meetings the two sides of the civil conflict were getting down to the brass tacks, as it were, of establishing the concord so magnificently celebrated in the wedding four days earlier. The situation was understandably tense, and by all accounts the Huguenot reaction to the attack on their chief representative in the political process was violent. The Florentine ambassador, for example, observed with alarm that the Huguenots threatened to storm 'the Louvre palace where Monsieur de Guise lived and to kill him in his chamber, driving back the royal guard and all those who might oppose them' (qtd Jouanna, 101). Prominent Huguenots such as Navarre, Condé, and Coligny's son-in-law Téligny confronted the King to demand justice, promising to take matters into their own hands should Charles not do so (Jouanna, 101). The King was faced with a rapidly mounting insurrection. The massacres were his response.

To invest Charles with sole responsibility for the massacres would be both unfair and historically misleading. In his dramatisation of the royal council convened by Catherine on the evening of 23 August to decide upon the royal course of action, Marlowe might have rendered Charles more passive than he actually was – 'What you determine I will ratify' (4.25), Charles tells his mother and Guise – but the scene captures the group nature of the decision. Marlowe is echoing the suspicions of many contemporary Protestant writers when he has Catherine declare the massacres to be the culmination of a trap that she and others have set for the Huguenots who have been drawn to Paris because of the wedding: 'Now have we got the fatal straggling deer / Within the compass of a deadly toil' (4.2–3), Catherine remarks to the other council members, 'And as we late decreed we may perform' (4). In contrast, modern historians generally agree that the council's intention was, in Arlette Jouanna's words, 'a remedial surgical excision that would remove a gangrenous part from the body social, in order to preserve the health of the rest' (Jouanna, 109). To remove the perceived Huguenot threat to royal authority, the Admiral and his followers were to be executed in what Charles would a few days later defend as an instance of the monarch's 'extraordinary justice' (Jouanna, 104–5). The surgery began before dawn on the morning of 24 August with attacks on the Admiral's residence and the Louvre, fanning out from there to the other locations in which Huguenot nobles were concentrated. Fifty or sixty Huguenots were targeted (Jouanna, 109; Garrisson, *La Saint-Barthélemy*, 131). The council decided that Navarre, Condé, and another Bourbon prince of blood, Montmorency-Thoré, would be the only ones spared (Garrisson, *La Saint-Barthélemy*, 93). The event quickly escaped royal control, however, and for the next six days Paris was engulfed by murderous religious violence that, according to modern historical estimates, left around 3,000 people dead (Jouanna, 3; Garrisson, *La Saint-Barthélemy*, 131). Ironically, during this second stage of the massacre the royal family barricaded themselves in the Louvre, afraid for their own safety. The body count more than tripled as the violence spread to provincial cities in the ensuing months (Jouanna, 142–3).

The massacre, Charles protests to his mother in scene 4, 'will be noted through the world / An action bloody and tyrannical' (5–6). Indeed, news of the event immediately created a storm of public responses, national and international. The international responses were predictably polarised along religious lines. The Pope celebrated the massacres with a special Mass and a commemorative medallion; Philip II of Spain publicly expressed his approval of Charles's efforts to extirpate heresy (Jouanna, 158). In Protestant England, with which France had just signed the defensive Treaty of Blois, the reaction was outrage. One of Elizabeth's councillors denounced the massacres as 'the worst crime since Jesus Christ came into the world' (qtd Jouanna, 160). Not all Catholics, however, greeted the bloodshed with rejoicing. Various Catholic states in Europe expressed their disapproval of the means Charles had employed against the Huguenots, even if they considered Protestantism to be heretical and credited Charles's public explanation of the massacres as a pre-emptive strike to prevent a Huguenot conspiracy against the French royal family (Jouanna, 159). The reaction was mixed among French Catholics as well. Calling them only 'learned men', François Hotman, whose eyewitness account of the massacres was translated and published in England in 1573, states that many Parisians 'said that they had read many histories, but in all memory of all ages they never heard of any such thing as this. They compared this case with the horrible doings of King Mithridates ... [who] caused a hundred and fifty thousand Romans to be slain' (*True and Plain Report*, 57). Conversely, in England outrage did not trump practical political considerations. Though she continued to support the Huguenot cause in other ways, Elizabeth did not back out of England's alliance with France, accepted Catherine de Medici's invitation to stand as godmother to Charles's daughter (also named Elizabeth), and continued to entertain the marriage proposal of the Duke of Alençon (Anjou had earlier been one of Elizabeth's suitors) (Guy, 282).

The first War of Religion had begun in 1562 with the massacre of a small group of French Protestants in the provincial town of Vassy. In the following decade, two more wars of religion were fought between Huguenot and Catholic forces, some semblance of peace and religious toleration finally being established in 1570 with the Edict of St Germain. The massacre of thousands of Huguenots in the French capital and provinces two years later set the inferno of civil war blazing again. The fire would not be extinguished until 1598, when Navarre as Henry IV promulgated the Edict of

Nantes. When *The Massacre at Paris* concludes, however, the fire is still burning as the last Valois king passes the torch to the first Bourbon. The year is 1589, and the second half of the play has skipped over the preceding fifteen years from Charles's death in 1574 and Anjou's coronation as Henry III in 1575 in order to focus on the period between 1587 and 1589, beginning with the Battle of Coutras in 1587 and ending with the assassinations first of Guise and his brother the Cardinal in 1588, and then of Henry III himself in 1589. These events form a cohesive unit, to maintain which, however, Marlowe has erased from his French history a number of significant figures and events, such as Henry's rebellious younger brother the Duke of Alençon and his death in 1584, and transposed others, such as the Duchess of Guise's affair with one of Henry III's minions.

The play cleverly bridges the temporal cleft between its two halves. At the end of scene 14, the scene in which Henry III is crowned, the Cardinal reports to Catherine that 'My brother Guise hath gathered a power of men, / Which, as he saith, to kill the Puritans, / But 'tis the house of Bourbon that he means' (54–6). Twelve years pass between this scene and scene 16, which takes place immediately before the Battle of Coutras in 1587, but the dramatic illusion of temporal continuity is maintained through what seems to be a continuity of action: if in scene 14 Guise was gathering an army, now in scene 16 it appears that he has put it in the field in conjunction with royal forces in opposition to 'the Puritans', specifically Navarre. '[T]hese our wars' (2), Navarre announces at the beginning of scene 16, are '[a]gainst the proud disturbers of the faith, / I mean the Guise, the Pope, and King of Spain' (3–4), and 'Guise for Spain hath now incensed the King / To send his power to meet us in the field' (14–15). This bit of dramatic prestidigitation is justified not only in terms of dramatic effectiveness but also as a way of registering the monotony of civil warfare, the seemingly static, endless looping of violence. Yet the play subtly registers the passage of time in scene 15, the scene in which Guise discovers his wife's affair with Maugiron. 'Am I grown old?' (24), Guise asks the Duchess, and '[i]s Guise's glory but a cloudy mist / In sight and judgement of thy lustful eye?' (29–30). The answer might well be 'yes'. Renowned for his beauty as a youth, during the third War of Religion in 1575 Guise was badly wounded on his left cheek and ear, leaving him with a disfiguring scar and the nickname 'le Balafré', or 'Scar-face' (Carroll, 223).

INTRODUCTION 9

Although the play scarcely mentions Alençon, the significance of his death in June 1584 to the historical narrative that the play is following cannot be underestimated. With Alençon's death, Navarre vaulted to the next in line to the French throne after Henry III. Navarre was no longer the heretical and rebellious 'petty king' (2.91) of 'but a nook of France' (2.90). Radical Catholics ('the Guise, the Pope, and King of Spain') were alarmed. The result was the formation of the Holy Union or Catholic League later in 1584. The Catholic League brought together powerful French Catholic forces at the municipal, provincial, national, and international levels in opposition to the prospect that the Protestant Navarre as heir presumptive represented: the final destruction of the religious unity of France. In December 1584 Guise and Spain signed the Treaty of Joinville, which declared Navarre ineligible to be king because of his Protestantism and affirmed both sides' commitment to the cause of eradicating heresy in France. Philip II backed his words with Spanish wealth, disbursing 50,000 escudos monthly to the League to finance its endeavours (Holt, 124). The governors of many French provinces joined the League, and in Paris middle-class Catholics organised themselves into the League cells that, combined, would flex their strength several years later on the Day of Barricades (Holt, 124–5). At whatever social and political levels they operated, however, all Leaguers were required to swear 'to use force and take up arms to the end that the holy church of God may be restored to its dignity and the true and holy Catholic religion' (qtd Holt, 126).

Directed against Navarre and French Protestantism though it may have been, the Catholic League also undermined the power and authority of the French monarchy. Faced with this threat, Henry III pre-emptively joined the League and in 1585, with the Treaty of Nemours, revoked all privileges that the Huguenots had gained through previous treaties (Holt, 126). The result was, once again, armed conflict between Protestant and Catholic forces: the eighth War of Religion. Navarre and Condé led the Protestant forces, while the King, seconded by Guise and the Duke of Joyeuse, led the Catholic armies. On 20 October 1587, Navarre's army engaged and defeated the forces led by Joyeuse at Coutras, in south-western France. Guise, though, offset this Catholic defeat with his victory against German mercenaries outside Chartres, 100 kilometres south-west of Paris, a month later (Holt, 128). Guise's victory was a mixed blessing for Henry. After having his victory over the German mercenaries snatched from him by Henry's negotiation of their withdrawal, Guise turned the forces under his command against the King, who then forbade him to return to Paris. Plotting a *coup d'état* against the King with the Parisians, Guise returned to Paris, ostensibly accompanied by only a few of his men, on 9 May (Carroll, 270–4). According to one modern historian, he 'was quickly recognized and there were shouts of "Long live Guise! Liberator of France, pillar of the Church, exterminator of heretics!"' (Carroll, 274). After ineffective negotiations between the two men, on 12 May, the Day of Barricades, Henry brought 6,000 French and Swiss troops into the city; the Parisians, organised by the Leaguers and supporting Guise, blocked off the streets with barricades. Henry's troops were routed in the ensuing street skirmishes, and Guise emerged as the day's hero by walking the streets unarmed and persuading both sides to stand down. Henry fled Paris for Chartres that evening after receiving intelligence that Guise had summoned reinforcements (Carroll, 275–9). Henry then convoked a general parliament for October, to be held in Blois (Garrisson, *Guerre civile*, 202). He dismissed his entire council on 8 September (Solnon, 349).

It is against this sombre historical backcloth that the play's concluding tragedies unfold: the assassinations of Guise and his brother, the Cardinal of Guise, followed by the assassination of Henry III himself. Henry had called the parliament at Blois, which opened on 16 October, as a means by which to reassert his sovereignty. The parliament was hostile, however, and pressed Henry both to commit to continued war against the Huguenots and to concede that sovereign power in France was vested not in the king alone but in the king and the people. Guise and the Cardinal were among the leaders of the parliamentary opposition (Solnon, 353–8). Henry was cornered, and, in the words of his biographer Jean-François Solnon, 'il ne lui restait que la force' (358). On the morning of 23 December Henry summoned Guise to attend a privy council meeting with the King; from the council room Guise was called into the King's adjoining private chambers, where he was cut down by seven of the King's royal guards and their captain, Loignac (Carroll, 290–1). The Cardinal had been summoned to the same privy council meeting as Guise and was arrested immediately after his brother's assassination (Solnon, 361). He was then murdered the following day, Christmas Eve, in his prison cell by six soldiers, each of whom was paid 200 livres for his service. His body, like his brother's, was then burnt (Carroll, 292). Henry also ordered the assassination of the third Guise brother, the Duke of

Mayenne, but he was forewarned and fled (Solnon, 362). After his brothers' deaths, Mayenne assumed control of the Holy League and continued its armed revolt against the King (Pitts, 137). The League, which still controlled Paris, denounced Henry as a tyrant and declared Mayenne 'Lieutenant-General of the State and the Crown of France' (Garrisson, *Guerre civile*, 204–5).

Earlier in 1588 Navarre had offered Henry armed support to defeat Guise's rebellion. Perhaps reluctant at that point to choose a side and hoping still for some sort of reconciliation with the forces of the Catholic League, Henry had declined (Pitts, 131–3). Now he accepted, and by the summer of 1589 his and Navarre's men were closing in on Paris. On 1 August 1589, however, fate would snatch the final victory from Henry's hands. From his château at St-Cloud, just outside Paris, Henry was preparing to besiege Paris while Navarre mopped up the provincial towns surrounding the city. That morning an unknown monk, Jacques Clément, arrived at the château and demanded an audience with the King, claiming to be carrying a letter from the captive first President of the Parisian Parliament, Achilles Harlay, who was a royalist. The unsuspecting Henry received Clément, who stabbed him in the stomach while he was reading the letter. Henry's guards immediately cut Clément down and defenestrated his body. Navarre was notified and was at Henry's bedside by 11 a.m. Although the surgeons attending Henry initially pronounced the wound light, Henry became feverish and died at 3 a.m. the next day, having confessed, prayed, pardoned his enemies and received absolution (Solnon, 378–81). Most contemporary writers and modern historians are convinced that Clément did not act on his own, implicating not only Clément's immediate religious superiors but also the very top of the Catholic League hierarchy, including the Duchess of Montpesier and the Duke of Mayenne (Solnon, 393).

Although it concludes Marlowe's play, the assassination of Henry III concluded nothing for the French. Before his death Henry declared Navarre to be his heir, but the Catholic League under Mayenne's leadership rejected his assumption of the crown and continued its armed resistance. To prevent the complete fragmentation of France, Navarre converted to Catholicism in 1593 and on 25 July of that year at the abbey of St-Denis, just outside Paris, was publicly received back into the Catholic Church (Pitts, 172). His coronation as Henry IV followed on 27 February 1594 at Chartres, and on 22 March the new monarch entered Paris peacefully, welcomed by the city's governor (Pitts, 179–81). By the end of 1595 even the Duke of Mayenne had made his peace with the first Bourbon king (Pitts, 195). Marlowe, of course, could not have foreseen, and was not alive to witness, this ironic twist of historical events or to pen it into his play. The play's mirroring structure, however, would prove to be prescient: like the Admiral, like the Guise brothers, like Henry III, Henry IV was in his turn assassinated in 1610.

SOURCES AND CRITICISM

The Massacre at Paris's sources have been well documented. In a series of three articles published during the 1940s, Paul Kocher presented detailed examinations of the play's reliance on contemporary pamphlet accounts of the 1572 massacre and the period between 1587 and 1589 with which the second half of the play is concerned. Kocher's analysis established that François Hotman's *A True and Plain Report of the Furious Outrages of France* (1573) is the major source for the first half of the play. Hotman, a Huguenot lawyer, wrote his account of the Paris massacre in Latin and published it in 1573 under the pseudonym of Ernest Varamund. The English translation from which Marlowe worked was published in the same year. A year later, Kocher notes, *A True and Plain Report* was reprinted without attribution as Book X of Jean Serres's *The Three Parts of Commentaries ... of the Civil Wars of France* (1574) (Kocher, 'François Hotman', 349–50). As Kocher's comparison of the play and the pamphlet demonstrates, the play follows the details of Hotman's account closely, even though it often departs from Hotman's chronology (these correspondences and departures have been documented in this edition's commentary notes). Marlowe may also have turned to other material, such as Arthur Golding's translation of Hotman's *The Life of ... Jasper Coligny* (1576) and Henry Estienne's *A Marvelous Discourse upon the Life, Deeds, and Behaviours of Katherine de Medici* (1575), for minor details in this half of the play (Kocher, 'François Hotman', 351). To this group of possible minor sources Jacques Ramel in 1979 added a collection of pamphlet accounts edited by Simon Goulart, the *Mémoires de l'état de France sous Charles neuvième* (1576) (Thomas and Tydeman, 253). For the post-massacre events dramatised by the play, the sources are, according to Kocher, far more diffuse. From his examination of 'some fifty contemporary pamphlets, Protestant and Catholic,

French and English', Kocher concludes that '[i]f Marlowe relied on any single account for these later scenes, it is indistinguishable among the welter of narrative and polemical pamphlets which the bloody progress of French affairs from 1572 to 1589 called forth in both France and England' ('Contemporary Pamphlet Backgrounds', 151). Subsequent scholarship has not contested Kocher's general assessment.

Subsequent scholarship has, however, contested the conclusions Kocher drew from his source studies. According to Kocher, 'Marlowe adopts current Protestant views about the situations and characters' of the events the play dramatises, for which reason the play is 'crass and violently partisan' ('Contemporary Pamphlet Backgrounds Part Two', 318). Marlowe is 'less concerned with historical accuracy than with dramatic effect. Most of the deviations from Hotman seem aimed at producing concentration, irony, the heaping up of the horrible, and the stirring of vengeful passions in the audience' (Kocher, 'François Hotman', 366). 'It seems clear', Kocher asserts, that Marlowe 'is consciously, and perhaps cynically, pandering to the most brutal appetites and prejudices of the Elizabethan spectator' ('François Hotman', 368). Kocher's damning verdict has often been repeated. Harry Levin calls the play 'a singularly crude and unpoetic potboiler' (84), for example; Wilbur Sanders dubs it a 'nasty piece of journalistic bombast' (22); and Frank Ardolino declares it 'a sensationalistic depiction of murderous historical events' (245). Nonetheless, this verdict does not represent a critical consensus. William Godshalk, for example, argues that '*The Massacre at Paris* is not a piece of Protestant propaganda' (101) but rather a 'well-balanced ... study where religion becomes the dominant means of disguising political aspiration' (100). In her landmark reassessment of the play's use of its sources, 'Marlowe's *Massacre at Paris*: A Reconsideration', Julia Briggs significantly qualifies Kocher's harsh conclusions. Arguing that 'the whole section of the play centring on the murder of the Guise is actually treated, not from the Huguenot viewpoint at all, but from the League viewpoint' (263), Briggs attributes to the play a critical irony that debunks the religious fanaticism, Protestant or Catholic, that motivates the play's violence. In her frequently cited essay on the play, 'Garbled Martyrdom in Christopher Marlowe's *The Massacre at Paris*', Kristen Poole concurs. 'Rather than offering an opportunity for the "intellect [to remain] inactive"', Poole contends, the play 'offers a profound interrogation into the mechanisms of social control and the dynamics of religious dissent'

(5). As Poole demonstrates, this interrogation is especially evident in the play's massacre scenes, which critically desacralise the murderous violence they depict by stripping the Huguenot victims of the veneer of martyrdom accorded them in such works as Foxe's *Acts and Monuments*.

Sensationalism and ideological bias have not been the only charges levelled at *The Massacre at Paris*. The play has also been accused of failing to shape its historical sources, of lacking dramatic structure, and of crude characterisation. If Kocher implies that Marlowe distorted his sources, Wilbur Sanders asserts that in *The Massacre at Paris* Marlowe 'is a kind of mechanical transcriber of events which are *given* ... The play is notable for a critical dependence on source material' (23). Few critics, however, have followed Sanders in his reduction of Marlowe to a kind of unthinking camera. The critical question, rather, has been how Marlowe shapes history in the play. Although characterising *The Massacre at Paris* as 'an unfeeling and rather tasteless play' (246), J. B. Steane argues that its representation of contemporary French history mirrors Shakespeare's representation of late medieval English history in his *Henry VI* plays: Charles IX is Henry VI, Henry III is Edward IV, Guise is Gloucester, and Navarre is Henry VII (245). Steane's historical equations are unnecessarily rigid, but the argument acquires a degree of plausibility in light of the facts that Marlowe's play contains a number of verbal echoes of the *Henry VI* plays, and that other writers, French as well as English, constructed mirroring parallels between medieval English history and contemporary French events. In 1588, for example, Jean Boucher published *Histoire tragique et mémorable de Pierre de Gaveston*, a translation of Thomas Walsingham's Latin history of the relationship between the English monarch Edward II and his favourite Piers Gaveston, as a way of attacking Henry III (Perry, 1063). Marlowe, of course, dramatises the same period of English history in *Edward II*, and David Potter has suggested that the 'ambiguity' of Marlowe's characterisation of Henry III in *The Massacre at Paris* reflects the ambiguity if not incoherence of Henry's reputation created by such polemics as Boucher's translation (Potter, 75).

Andrew Kirk, in contrast, argues that critics have been too quick to see *The Massacre at Paris* as English history in French costume. More precisely, Kirk observes, critics have found the play to be confused because it does not reproduce the same providentialist patterns according to which Tudor historians wrote English history.

For Elizabethans, however, France provided a distinct, 'other', historical topos, a place of instability (gendered feminine) that presented an opportunity for the man who could impose order on it – in short, a Machiavellian topos in which providential causality could be set aside and alternative modes of historiography explored. Marlowe, according to Kirk, dramatises French history according to this alternative, Machiavellian mode of historiography, 'delineating France as a place requiring the inscription of stable, masculine authority, a role assumed by both Navarre and Guise' (209). Richard Hillman urges the adoption of a more complex, 'intertextual' (9) understanding of the play's relationship to French history as a 'field of symbolic exchange relations' (11) in which self and other construct and deconstruct each other. As Rick Bowers puts it,

> In presenting recent French history, Christopher Marlowe's *The Massacre at Paris* presents a mirror in which to stare with morbid fascination and a less-than-secure sense of English satisfaction. After all, the play puts its audience within the minds of the perpetrators, risking dangerously reflexive associations, conflicting possibilities, treasonous imaginings. (139)

Critics have also singled out the play's dramatic structure as a major flaw. According to these critics, the structure fails to shape its historical material into a unified whole, producing a broken-backed play in which the dramatisation of the event announced in the title seems to have little if anything to do with the events that follow. H. S. Bennett, for example, asserts that the play 'deals in a shambling pedestrian way with events spread over many years, and certainly does not escape a familiar weakness of the historical drama – considerable structural incoherence' (174), a judgement echoed by Michel Poirier, who decries 'the absence of a unified coherent structure' (166) in the play. Later critics have dissented from this common verdict. William Godshalk contends that '*The Massacre* is a well-balanced play, and Marlowe has carefully selected and molded the material he gathered from the histories of contemporary France' (84). Roy Eriksen argues that the play is unified through the repetition of 'textual patterns' that 'convey the idea that history repeats itself, while providing the sort of enclosure proper to tragedy' (52). Observing the similarities between the play's dramatisation of the murder of religious figures such as the preacher Léran during the massacre and the murder of the Cardinal in the play's second half, Briggs argues that 'The play's structure thus turns on the ironic relation between the massacre of the Huguenots and the murder of the Guise brothers, an event that was frequently referred to as a massacre by League pamphleteers' (268). Deats has extended Briggs's argument to all the play's major characters in order to argue that the play operates in an 'interrogative mode' (203) that 'undermines a simplistic dichotomy between good guys and bad guys' (201).

As Deats's comments suggest, critics who condemn the play for its structural weakness often single out its characterisation as another of its aesthetic flaws. Wilbur Sanders, for example, argues that 'Guise is never sufficiently characterised to be able to exist in any social or political *context*. Indeed there is no social or political context in this play – only a chaos of religious platitudes and nationalist war-cries, gigantic self-assertions of gigantic non-entities' (32). Critics aiming to rehabilitate the play have defended the play's characterisation, mainly by arguing that it exposes characters of all stripes – Guise, Henri, Navarre – to be Machiavellians. Thus Briggs describes the difference between Guise and Henry as 'hot versus cold Machiavellianism' (265), adding Navarre to the list as 'yet another political operator, exploiting religious fervour to bring him one step nearer the crown' (273). Among later critics such as Briggs a critical consensus of sorts has emerged that that the play's characters are not as crude as earlier critics claimed and that the political context does make sense of much of their action. Nonetheless, I will suggest, the play's characters are fundamentally incoherent, as Guise's dying words illustrate. As with the broken-backed nature of the play, this incoherence is not an aesthetic flaw but rather a feature of what I will discuss below as the play's traumatic aesthetics.

THE MASSACRE AT PARIS, TRAUMA, AND MEMORY

In *The Massacre at Paris* the relationship between trauma and memory is central. The play's sensorily shocking staging of mass murder warps historical memory and aesthetic form. As we have seen, until recently the critical consensus has been that the play is indisputably defective aesthetically and morally. Contemporary trauma theory, however, provides a critical framework that renders the play's putative defects more intelligible as part of an alternative aesthetics that breaks rather than valorises conventional aesthetic qualities such as wholeness and sense.

Charles signals the importance of the force of memory early on in the play when in scene 4 he declares to his mother, 'Madam, it will be noted through the world / An action bloody and tyrannical'

(5-6), before giving his consent to the massacre. The numerous pamphlet accounts generated by the international uproar over the massacre do in fact seek to memorialise the event in Charles's specific terms, 'bloody and tyrannical'. Hotman, the play's major source, sums the massacre up as 'This butcherly slaughter of Paris' (*True and Plain Report*, 64). If Hotman's pamphlet emphasises the event's bloodiness, then Goulart's *Mémoires* emphasises its tyranny, suggesting, as Robert Kingdon puts it, that 'these massacres had been caused by a government become so authoritarian that it had gone berserk and become a tyranny ruthlessly intent on extinguishing traditional rights of individuals' (5). Hotman and Goulart published their works soon after 1572, and, as the historian John Guy notes, the Elizabethan government's 'moral outrage was tempered by *realpolitik*' (282). Nonetheless, the massacre was still fresh in English memories in 1586, when George Whetstone in *The English Myrror* asked,

> where was there a more savage cruelty ever committed than the massacre of Paris, where ... many a thousand innocent and fearless Protestants in Paris and other cities of France were cruelly murdered, which monstrous massacre (although many other treacherous murders in France reproach the Papists with the extremest name of cruelty) is remembered with the blame and exclamation of the cruelest Pagans in the world. (96)

In a historical period full of bloody religious violence, then, the massacre at Paris was memorable for its scope, its extreme brutality, and its shocking political implications. It was what trauma theorists have labelled as 'an extreme historical event'.

Many accounts of this extreme historical event attempt to contain its traumatic impact within the framework of tragedy. In *The Discoverie of a Gaping Gulf* (1579), for instance, John Stubbes elaborates upon the theatre metaphor in his depiction of Catherine de Medici's guiding role in the events: 'In this tragedy she played her part naturally and showed how she governs all France ... [T]he mother as setter forth of this earnest game stood holding the book (as it were) upon the stage and told her children and every other player what he should say; the last act was very lamentable' (sig. B4ᵛ). In Marlowe's play, several characters employ the theatre metaphor: in scene 2, for example, Guise commands the soldier whom he has hired to assassinate the Admiral to 'come thou forth and play thy tragic part' (27), and as he dies Henry III declaims 'Valois's line ends in my tragedy' (24.93). As lamentable as the events dramatised by Marlowe's play are, however, the conventional Aristotelian qualities of tragedy are precisely the aesthetic criteria that the play rejects in its dramatisation of French history. The play is an instance of what Michael Rothberg and Dominick LaCapra call 'traumatic realism'. 'Traumatic realism', Rothberg writes,

> develops out of and in response to the demand for documentation that an extreme historical event poses to those who would seek to understand it ... Traumatic realist texts ... search for a form of documentation beyond direct reference and coherent narrative but do not fully abandon the possibility of some kind of reference and some kind of narrative. (100–1)

LaCapra argues that 'traumatic realism ... differs from stereotypical conceptions of mimesis and enables instead an often disconcerting exploration of disorientation, its symptomatic dimensions, and possible ways of responding to them' (186). The extreme historical events that are the play's focus, at least for its first half, demand representational strategies that go beyond the referentiality or simple fidelity to what Marlowe might have considered the historical facts, and those representational strategies do not conform to conventional mimetic or historiographical expectations. The play dramatises history as, in Cathy Caruth's words, 'a history of trauma' (17).

The play's traumatic history emerges out of a cultural context fractured by what Jonathan Baldo in relation to Shakespeare's *Henry V* has termed 'wars of memory' (133). 'Collective memory', Baldo writes,

> is an extension of the kinds of power and even brutality exercised in war. Wars of memory are not bloodless but intimately tied to the loss of lives and limbs. Control over how a nation remembers a momentous event like a war is almost as significant as the outcome of the war itself, given how crucial memory is for the legitimation and exercise of power. (133)

The struggle to control how the momentous event of the St Bartholomew's Day massacre was remembered, in the context of an ongoing civil war, was intense: the various parties involved in or witnesses to the massacre articulated multiple, contradictory narratives within which to frame and make sense of the trauma of this early modern 'extreme historical event'. Impinging upon these narratives, as upon Marlowe's play, was not only the imperative to remember but also the pressure to forget.

Forgetting in this context can be seen to operate on a number of levels. As has been mentioned, before her marriage to Navarre,

Margaret had a love affair with Guise and was rumoured to have had incestuous relations with her brother, Anjou (Solnon, 85-8). The material is there, then, for a version of the massacre that places it in the generic frame of a love tragedy (with possible complications worthy of Ford). *Edward II* demonstrates that Marlowe found the relationship between private sexual desires and public history worth sustained consideration. Nonetheless, none of the pamphlet accounts of the massacre recognised by modern scholars as sources for Marlowe invokes such a frame, and if Marlowe encountered the information regarding Margaret's love entanglements in other sources, he forgot about it. *The Massacre at Paris* begins with the marriage of Margaret to Navarre. Margaret's other two Henrys are in the vicinity (Guise takes the stage in scene 2, Anjou could be on stage in the first scene and definitely enters in the fourth). No mention is made of the erotic dynamics between the four. Indeed, it is not Guise himself but 'The Guise's brother, and the Duke Dumaine' (1.47) who, the Admiral tells the bridegroom Navarre, 'did storm at these your nuptial rites, / Because the house of Bourbon now comes in' (48-9). Roughly a century later, the framing potential of this material unknown to (forgotten for) or forgotten by Marlowe would surface in dramatic form in Nathaniel Lee's *Massacre of Paris* (1690), based on a source that post-dates Marlowe. Significantly, however, according to H. J. Oliver neither Lee's play nor the *Duke of Guise* (1682), a play Lee wrote in collaboration with Dryden, 'shows any indebtedness to Marlowe' (Oliver, li). Forgetting, as well as remembering, is a transgenerational cultural process.

One might argue that at this level, at the level of the intersection of illicit sexual desire and traumatic history, the forgetting is collective and unconscious, the possible love tragedy narrative being displaced or repressed by attempts to place the traumatic events in seemingly more serious frames. One such frame, which finds place in the contemporary pamphlet literature but is ignored by Marlowe, is that of personal revenge tragedy. Contemporary pamphlet accounts often suggest that the event that triggered the massacre, the assassination attempt on the Admiral, could at least in part have been motivated by Guise's desire to avenge the death of his father, whose assassination was believed by Guise and others to have been masterminded by the Admiral. Historically, in 1564 and again in 1566 Charles IX held official inquiries into the matter. The first concluded by suspending judgement on the Admiral's guilt and commanding an end to the armed conflict between the Guises and the Montmorency family to which the Admiral belonged (Carroll, 172). At the royally mandated conclusion of the second inquiry, the Admiral publicly swore his innocence, and his Guise accuser, the Cardinal of Lorraine, was compelled to exchange a kiss of peace with him (Carroll, 174–5). Immediately before commencing his narrative of the marriage between Navarre and Margaret, Hotman recounts another such attempt to induce forgetting. Intending to quench the 'old enmity between the Guisians and the Admiral, whereby it was to be doubted that perilous contentions would arise in the realm of France' (*True and Plain Report*, 26), Charles 'pronounced the Admiral not guilty of the death of the Duke of Guise, wherewith he was charged by the young Duke of Guise and his kinsmen' (26). Placed within the frame of revenge tragedy, then, Guise's assassination attempt upon and subsequent murder of the Admiral could acquire the status of what Francis Bacon calls 'a kind of wild justice' (347) that defies royal pressure to forget, a Hamlet-like act of remembering in the face of enforced collective amnesia. Yet the play does not invoke this frame either, although the assassination attempt's juxtaposition with the atrocities of which it might be seen to have been the cause might register as an implicit rejection of the revenge narrative as a solution to trauma, a silent affirmation of Bacon's assertion that 'a man that studieth revenge keeps his own wounds green, which otherwise would heal' (348). According to Navarre in scene 1, the 'malice of his [Guise's] envious heart' (29) is not directed against the Admiral in particular but 'all the Protestants' (30) and 'the house of Bourbon' (49). In his soliloquy in scene 2, Guise makes no mention of his father but confesses his motivation to be 'A royal seat, a sceptre, and a crown' (103). After the Admiral's corpse is thrown into the street in scene 5, Guise 'stamps on thy lifeless bulk' (41), a gesture appropriate to a revenger but not explicitly described as such: Guise performs this action 'in despite of thy [the Admiral's] religion' (40). It is an act of profanation, not revenge. Whatever Guise's motivations are, the play does not allow them to crystallise into a single, identifiable motive that might be placed within a narrative frame such as revenge tragedy. In Marlowe's *Tamburlaine*, tragic frames are explicitly broken: Zenocrate's troping of Bajazeth and Zabina's fate as *de casibus* tragedy, for example, is overtly rejected by her maid Anippe and reworked by Tamburlaine in his 'sights of power' (1.5.2.410) speech. In *The Massacre at Paris*, tragic frames are silently not chosen or, to put it more strongly, actively forgotten in order to

INTRODUCTION   21

privilege an incoherence that refuses to bring trauma into narrative order. The most remarkable indication of *The Massacre at Paris*'s refusal to reduce trauma to order, however, is the silence about the massacre that follows its dramatisation. Scenes 1–13, roughly half of the play, are concerned with the massacre. The first four scenes provide the massacre's immediate context, while the first half of scene 13 provides the only staging of its aftermath, in the form of the death of a guilt-stricken Charles. The scenes in which the massacre is staged, 5–12, are striking for their swiftness, their brutality, and not least for the fact that a bell, the infamous tocsin of contemporary pamphlet accounts, rings for the massacre's duration. Scenes 6, 7, 8, and 12 are all under 15 lines. They are as formulaic as the battle scenes in *Tamburlaine*, but in stark contrast they are shorn of hyperbolic rhetoric and move straight to the point of the action: Guise and/or his followers chase down a Huguenot or group of Huguenots, taunt them, and then kill them. A crude indicator of the insignificance of words in comparison to action is the fact that in scene 6, for example, the opening stage direction, 'The Guise enters again, with all the rest, with their swords drawn, chasing the Protestants', contains more words than the entire scene's dialogue, which consists of Guise shouting '*Tuez, tuez, tuez*! / Let none escape, murder the Huguenots!' (1–2), followed by Anjou's 'Kill them, kill them!' (3). Throughout scenes 5–12 the setting shifts rapidly from one location to another – there is no unity of place in these scenes; it does not obey the aesthetic decorum of classical or neoclassical tragedy – to create a whirlwind of action.

Scenes 5–12 are full of swiftly executed instances of violence. 'Dearly beloved brother', the Guise intones as he prepares to murder the preacher Léran, 'thus 'tis written' (7.5), which is followed immediately by the stage direction 'He stabs him' (7.5 SD). In the next scene Seroune pleads with Montsoreau to 'let me pray unto my God!' (8.13). 'Then take this with you' (14) is Montsoreau's reply, again immediately followed by the stage direction 'Stab him' (8.14 SD). The massacre scenes stab at all their audience's senses, and senses of decorum. 'The watchword being given', Guise informs Catherine before setting the massacre in motion, 'a bell shall ring, / Which, when they hear, they shall begin to kill, / And never cease until that bell shall cease' (4.36–8). And the bell does ring: after the Admiral's murder and mutilation in scene 5 at 'the entrance of this massacre' (5.12), the bell begins to toll, and it does not stop until the conclusion of scene 9, when the Guise commands 'now stay that bell that to the devil's matins rings' (86). The octavo, 'bad' because considered a memorial reconstruction by actors who performed the play, contains at the appropriate place in scene 5 the stage direction 'The ordnance being shot off, the bell tolls' (5.59 SD), and the loud ringing of the bell must be counted as an integral part of the performance. Over this noise the actors were required to shout, and the cry the audience would have heard both at the commencement of the massacre and at its conclusion at the end of scene 12, when the echoes of the bell's clapper were still ringing in their ears, would have been '*Tuez, tuez, tuez!*' (6.1), '*Tuez, tuez, tuez*, let none escape!' (12.7). The massacre scenes of the play's first half, then, qualify as what LaCapra calls a 'disconcerting exploration of disorientation' (186), forcing themselves upon the audience's senses visually and aurally.

The second half of the play's silence about the massacre is therefore almost as audible as the tocsin's clapper. Robert Kingdon observes that, in *Le Réveille-Matin*'s (1573) account of the terms of peace accepted at La Rochelle after the fighting triggered by the massacre, it is noted that one of the clauses of the royal edict 'orders all memory of the massacres to be extinguished and no legal proceedings growing out of them to be allowed' (86). The first article in Arthur Golding's translation of 'The Edict or Proclamation set forth by the French King upon the pacifying of the troubles in France ... Read and published in the presence of the said King, sitting in his Parliament, the xiiii day of May, 1576' is 'That the remembrance of all things past as well on the one side as on the other, during and since the troubles that have happened in our said realm, and by occasion of them, shall lie quenched and dead, as things that had never been done' (4). Tyrannical though Henry's imperative to forget might appear, it expresses a desire to destroy memory that became official French government policy. In *Forgetting Differences: Tragedy, Historiography, and the French Wars of Religion*, Andrea Frisch suggests that 'The impossibility of either eliminating the Huguenots or converting them seems to have led beyond the traditional alternatives of clemency or vengeance and towards the development of a rhetoric of *oubliance*' (35) that culminated in the Edict of Nantes (1598), which 'consolidated a long series of royal efforts to reorient the status of the civil war in public discourse, from an occasion for juridical vengeance, retribution, and restitution (or, alternatively, clemency and pardon) to an atrocity that utterly exceeds the grasp of legislation, and that is ultimately best forgotten' (51). The reorientation had long-lasting if only partial effects: '[E]very French citizen is required to have forgotten the St. Bartholomew's Day massacres' ('What is a Nation', qtd Frisch, 11), asserted Ernest Renan in 1882.

The policy and practice of *oubliance* frame even the most trenchant acts of remembering: Hotman begins his account of the massacre with the declaration that 'It were to be wished that the memory of the fresh slaughters and of that butcherly murdering that hath lately been committed in a manner in all the towns of France were utterly put out of the minds of men' (*True and Plain Report*, 5). In its second half, the play seems to follow Henry's royal command and enact Hotman's resistance to remembering the massacre. Although with the exception of the defunct Charles IX the major characters in the second half are those of the first half, all of whom were involved in the massacre in some way, none of them mentions the massacre directly and specifically, even when presented with the occasion to do so. Indeed, in several instances characters veer so close to the massacre in their discourse that their failure to refer to it is conspicuous. In scene 14, the scene of Anjou's coronation as Henry III on 13 February 1575 in Reims Cathedral, Guise's brother the Cardinal informs Catherine that 'My brother Guise hath gathered a power of men, / Which, as he saith, to kill the Puritans, / But 'tis the house of Bourbon that he means' (54–6). The Cardinal's quick movement here from talk of killing Puritans to dynastic conflict raises the massacre's ghost only to dissipate it in the vapour of a deliberate deception. As he prepares for war against Henry III several scenes later, Navarre declaims against 'the Guise, the Pope, and King of Spain' (16.4) who have instigated the conflict in order to 'rent our true religion from this land' (6) and then declares that 'The power of vengeance now encamps itself / Upon the haughty mountains of my breast, / Plays with her gory colours of revenge' (20–2). Here, if anywhere, is Navarre's opportunity to invoke the names of the victims of the massacre at Paris, to locate the massacre as the event for which he will now pursue his revenge as leader of the French Protestants. Instead, in lines whose strained decorum recalls the violent poetry of the *Tamburlaine* plays, Navarre anticipates his victory in the upcoming battle, comparing vengeance's gory colours to 'leaves of boasting green / That change their colour when the winter comes, / When I shall vaunt as victor in revenge' (23–5).

It is much later in the play, however, during the scene of Guise's murder, that the avoidance of specific reference to the 1572 massacre is most noticeable. Having commanded Guise's assassination, Henry III gloats over the body in a speech whose movement, like the movement of the Cardinal's earlier in the play, raises the memory of the massacre only to dissipate it. Henry begins by commanding Guise's soul, 'Surcharged with guilt of thousand massacres' (21.89), to 'sink away to hell!' (90). These lines are followed by what seems to be a gesture of remembrance and a confession of guilt: 'in remembrance of those bloody broils / To which thou didst allure me, being alive, / And here in presence of you all, I swear' (91–3). But the line break disappoints. What Henry swears is 'I ne'er was King of France until this hour. / This is the traitor that hath spent my gold / In making foreign wars and civil broils' (94–6). Line by line Henry's speech erases the seeming specificity of the word 'massacre', at first subsuming it within thousands of other massacres then conflating it with 'bloody' 'civil' broils in general; his oath abruptly shifts attention from remembrance to the present moment of his own personal triumph. 'There can have been few occasions in drama', Wilbur Sanders pointedly comments, 'when erring man has been able to lock so many skeletons in the one capacious cupboard' (34).

The massacre staged in the play's first half, then, functions in the second as a traumatic black hole whose gravitational pull bends the characters' discourse into circles of oblique attraction that leave the massacre unspoken while registering its dark density. In psychoanalysts Abraham and Torok's metapsychological terminology, the play's main characters are 'cryptophores' (157) whose reality is structured by complicity in a crime whose encryption renders it unspeakable. Unspeakable and necessarily rejected from constructions of 'reality', the encrypted massacre is registered in the play's dramatic structure as well as in the characters' discourse. As we have seen, many of the play's earlier critics have held its dramatic structure to be one of its more egregious aesthetic flaws. Later critics have revised this assessment. Most relevant here, however, is Richard Hillman's recent approach to the play's structural problem in terms of memory. Hillman contests the evaluation of critics such as Bennett by arguing that the play is structured as a pointed act of remembering that counters the forgetting implicit in Holy League pamphlets and literary works such as Pierre Matthieu's *La Guisiade* (1589), which troped Guise's assassination in 1588 as the massacre that originated the cycle of violence leading to Henry III's assassination in 1589. By juxtaposing the two temporally distant events of the

1572 massacre and the events leading up to Guise's assassination in 1588, according to Hillman, the play recovers or decrypts the massacre as the source of the trauma of recent French history.

> [W]hen Marlowe reaches back in time to attach to the Guise's recent death the event qualifying, in Protestant eyes, as the true and original 'massacre' – indeed, according to *le Tocsin contre les massacrvers*, as the primordial 'tragoedie', he imposes upon Matthieu the supplement of providential history stretching backwards, as well as further forwards. (Hillman, 87)

Yet if Marlowe's play is an act of remembering, it is a strange one, for the juxtaposition central to Hillman's claim is also a disjunction. In order to unearth and represent the massacre as trauma, the play must violate one of tragedy's cardinal aesthetic criteria, structural unity or, in Aristotelian terminology, the unity of action. The play's dramatic structure quite emphatically does not present the massacre as the visible cause or origin of the characters' subsequent actions. Although one might speculate about the massacre's effects on the play's characters, on the political situation in which they find themselves, or on French history in general, within the play's dramatic structure the massacre is largely inconsequential. With the ascension of Anjou to the throne in scene 14 the play seems to begin anew, establishing the origins for the conflict between Henry III and Guise in the conflict between the Duke and Henry's minions and then developing that conflict as a revenge tragedy culminating in the double catastrophe of the two protagonists' deaths. Here the frameworks of love tragedy and revenge tragedy *are* invoked: having discovered his wife's affair with Henry's minion Maugiron in scene 15 and been taunted by Henry about it in scene 17, Guise in revenge instigates Maugiron's murder, which happens in scene 19; Henry's assassination of the increasingly threatening Guise in scene 21 is, in dramatic time, almost immediately avenged as Guise's brother Dumaine commissions Henry's assassination in scene 23 and the friar carries it out in the following, final scene of the play. These intertwined frameworks serve only to consolidate the play's second half as an independent unity and deepen the disjunction between it and the dramatisation of the massacre in the play's first half. In this dramatic scheme, Navarre's arrival to the French throne is much like Fortinbras's arrival to the Danish throne in *Hamlet*.

The play, then, is undeniably 'broken-backed' in spite of the clever dramatic bridging between scenes 14 and 16 remarked upon earlier. Yet it is in precisely this breaking of causal unity that the play registers the massacre as historical trauma that escapes what Eriksen calls the 'enclosure proper to tragedy' (52). Cathy Caruth comments that 'For history to be a history of trauma means that it is referential precisely to the extent that it is not fully perceived as it occurs; or to put it somewhat differently, that a history can be grasped only in the very inaccessibility of its occurrence' (17–18). In *The Massacre at Paris* that inaccessibility takes the form of resistance to historiographical and aesthetic perception, resistance to the rationalising Epimethean gaze that would delimit the massacre as the cause of a definable series of effects leading to historical and aesthetic closure.

The role of witness into which the play's resistance casts its audience is not a comfortable one. The play provides no consoling, suturing narrative. It does not allow the audience to remain a distant, objective observer: in its first half it presents on stage, in the now of the dramatic moment and before their very eyes, an event known to the audience only through the reported action of pamphlet prose; yet the audience is jettisoned into the acting out of the traumatic past only to be as helpless to stop the unfolding events as the massacre's victims. In the aftermath of the massacre, the play positions Elizabeth and Elizabethans not only as friendly allies of the Huguenots but also as potential victims in the struggle against the international Catholic intrigue headed by the Guisians, the Pope, and Spain. The play's allusions to England raise anxiety-provoking memories of recent assassination plots against Elizabeth, the Armada (Roberts, 434), and consequently fears of the importation to England of 'a program of Protestant genocide' that the 'Spanish army appeared to have institutionalized ... in the Low Countries' (MacKenzie, 85) in the period. Indeed, in 1583 evidence surfaced to place Guise at the head of a projected Spanish invasion of England (Parker, 169). Henry III touches on these English anxieties as he declaims over Guise's dead body in scene 21: Guise did 'draw a sort of English priests / From Douai to the seminary at Reims / To hatch forth treason 'gainst their natural queen' (97–9) and did 'cause the King of Spain's huge fleet / To threaten England and to menace me' (100–1). In the play's final scene Henry summons the English agent in order to 'send my sister England news' (24.51) of the attempt on his life and 'give her warning of her treacherous foes' (52). 'The explicit didactic lesson for English audiences' in the 1590s is clear, according to David Bevington: there 'is the immediate danger of a comparable outrage at the English court', and 'such a massacre can happen in England' (204).

If they are positioned as potential victims, though, Elizabeth and the Elizabethan audience are also positioned as potential perpetrators of trauma. In scene 18, Navarre declares that he will 'with the Queen of England join my force / To beat the papal monarch from our lands' (18.15–16). After issuing his warning to Elizabeth to beware of assassins, Henry additionally commands the English agent to tell Elizabeth 'that I hope to live, / Which if I do, the papal monarch goes to wrack' (24.58–9), presumably with English aid. Although he soon realises that his hope is vain, Henry nonetheless urges those around him to respond to his fatal wounding by committing further atrocities: he 'bids thee whet thy sword on Sixtus' bones, / That it may keenly slice the Catholics' (99–100) and to 'Fire Paris' (103). As Navarre and Henry III position them, then, Elizabeth and the Elizabethans are either potential victims of atrocity or collaborators in its perpetuation. More frighteningly, they are both: active complicity in the perpetuation of trauma is one possible response, the response overwhelmingly encouraged by the play's characters, to their potential victimisation. Briggs argues that the audience can respond to the massacre scenes in the play's first half either by sympathising with the massacre's victims or by identifying with the murderers, as if they were 'witnessing an execution or participating in a lynching' (278). Poole rejects the latter alternative: 'To imagine an English audience identifying with the Catholic murderers (a possibility presented by Briggs) is difficult; on the contrary, in watching these scenes of massacre, an English audience would have been more likely to have seen themselves in the faces of the victims' (19). Through the bellicose speeches of Navarre and Henry, however, the play links the two positions. If the audience identifies with the victims, then paradoxically it is later encouraged to identify with or desire to adopt the same position as the victims' murderers – the perpetrators of religious violence.

Henry's injunction to 'Fire Paris' might have vexed an Elizabethan London audience's attempt to play the role of witness with feelings of insecurity as well as complicity. In commanding the holocaust of Paris, which might be considered to be an act of revenge for his Parisian subjects' treasonous defiance of him, Henry seems to be forgetting once again his responsibility for and participation in the massacre at Paris dramatised in the play's first half. This final moment of foregrounded amnesia, which culminates the second half of the play's silence about the massacre and the massacre's strange inconsequentiality, must have resonated deeply if not consciously with its Elizabethan audience, both troubling their claim to innocence and touching on their own ambiguous positions in the 'wars of memory' concerning the massacre played out in the English cultural consciousness. Although it provoked protest from Elizabeth when it happened, the massacre was as inconsequential to Elizabeth's French foreign policy as it is in the play. To retain the position of ethically innocent witness, Marlowe's audience would need strenuously to forget such culturally significant matters in Anglo-French relations as the 1562 Hampton Court treaty by which Elizabeth exploited Huguenot needs in order to redress the loss of Calais, the much decried absence of effective English military intervention in support of the Huguenots, and Elizabeth's notorious marriage negotiations with Anjou as well as Alençon, negotiations that the massacre did nothing to impede (Guy, 267–8; Neale, 224–34). Here we can recall historian John Guy's remark that 'The Massacre of St. Bartholomew caused an estrangement in Anglo-French relations ... But moral outrage was tempered by *realpolitik*' (282).

Through the sensory assault of the staging of the trauma of the massacre as well as through the subsequent collective silence about it, however, it is precisely the amnesia of *realpolitik* that the play has invited its audience to interrogate. Such interrogation was risky, potentially placing the Elizabethan subject in treasonous opposition to her or his sovereign through the very act of bearing witness. As Rick Bowers notes, John Stubbes, 'along with his publisher, was publicly dismembered in the marketplace at Westminster' (133) for opposing Elizabeth's marriage negotiations with Alençon in a pamphlet, *The Discoverie of a Gaping Gulf* (1597), that invoked the memory of the massacre to bolster its opposition. The audience of *The Massacre at Paris* would be required to forget Stubbes's severed right hand in order to forget that 'the acts of violence perpetrated in *The Massacre at Paris* were perpetrated by Christian monarchs and nobles not unlike their own' (Bowers, 139). Marlowe, Bowers contends, 'rehearses French atrocity and then veers it toward England where authority too asserts itself over "treacherous foes" through official public displays of violence' (139).

While the play raises its Elizabethan audience's anxiety by positioning its members as potential victims of atrocity, then, it nonetheless does not give that audience the moral luxury of complete identification with the massacre's victims or the sense of safety that might come from self-identification as English. Rather, it presses the audience to recognise its ambivalent relation to and even complicity in the historical trauma it dramatises. *The Massacre at Paris* is not only an act of remembering: by breaking the criteria of tragic aesthetics and historiography, by obtruding incoherence, it also directs attention to the amnesia necessary to constitute history and the ethically simple subject positions from which individuals might attempt to perform the role of outraged witnesses of history's atrocities.

THE *MASSACRE AT PARIS* AND RELIGIOUS TOLERATION

The topic of religious toleration is a major concern in several of Marlowe's plays. *2 Tamburlaine*, for example, begins with Islamic and Christian forces attempting to surmount their religious differences in order to put an end to the armed conflict between them. *The Jew of Malta* is driven by the mutually intolerant behaviour of Jew and Christian. Marlowe seems to have been fascinated by religiously explosive situations, and it is no surprise, then, that the French Wars of Religion should engage his interest. The wars were extreme examples of the horrible consequences of religious intolerance, and some modern scholars have suggested that our own modern notions of religious toleration had their beginnings in the political thinking generated by the Wars of Religion (Kaplan, 1–8). As we will see, there are significant differences between early modern and modern understandings of religious toleration. Nonetheless, the idea was not unthinkable, and Marlowe and his European contemporaries had examples of religiously tolerant states in the Ottoman Empire and Poland, both of which lurk in the background of *The Massacre at Paris*. Like the memory of the 1572 massacres in the latter half of the play, religious toleration in *The Massacre at Paris* is most conspicuous by its absence. This absence, however, haunts the play from its beginning. As has been noted, earlier critics have dismissed the play as a piece of Protestant propaganda, that is, as an example of religiously intolerant discourse. Certainly, the play is full of religiously intolerant discourse – of both the Protestant and Catholic varieties, it should be added. Indeed, as Brian Walsh has argued in his recent reading of the subtle differences among the terms 'Lutheran', 'Puritan', and 'Huguenot' in the play, the fissures of intolerance may be found even within the discourses of Protestantism. '[T]he complexity of pan-Protestantism as an ideal is on vivid display here', Walsh contends, 'and this complexity haunts

The Massacre at Paris and its polyvalent discourse of naming forms of Protestantism' (36). Walsh concludes that the play 'does not exhibit the viability of toleration in any sense of the term' (37). Overall, the play's staging of religious intolerance is framed by failed rhetorical strategies to defuse religious difference and missed opportunities for religious concord. The result is not a piece of religious propaganda, however, but rather a bleak dramatisation of the failure of nascent discourses of religious toleration.

Intellectual historians have generally considered religious tolerance to be an invention of the Enlightenment, singling out Pierre Bayle's *Commentaire philosophique sur ces paroles de Jésus Christ: Contrain-les d'entrer* (1686) and John Locke's *Letter Concerning Toleration* (1689) 'as providing for the first time a philosophical basis for religious toleration in the modern sense' (Kaplan, 334). Earlier scholarship, such as Joseph Lecler's *Toleration and the Reformation* (1960), W. K. Jordan's *The Development of Religious Toleration in England* (1932; 1965), and Quentin Skinner's magisterial *The Foundations of Modern Political Thought* (1978), sought to document the idea's roots in Erasmian humanism and strands of Lutheran thought. While conceding and often seeking to extend the work of these previous scholars, however, recent studies of the history of religious toleration have stressed the difference between its pre-modern and modern forms. Cary Nederman contends that 'medieval writing about toleration promotes doctrines standing well outside the now-standard modern, liberal vision ... Whereas the latter believed tolerance to be among the worthy goals of human life, the former held toleration to follow from the unfortunate limits imposed on human beings by their common nature' (9). In early modern Europe, Alexandra Walsham argues, toleration was

> a strategy to ensure survival and to facilitate restoration to exclusive rule rather than an end in and of itself. When the mantle of authority settled on religious dissidents and rebels, they all too often set aside the rousing rhetoric of liberty they had hitherto employed ... Alternatively, toleration might be a tactical step towards reunification, an interim solution to the problem of religious disunity, an instrument for re-establishing communal peace and political concord. (3–4)

The numerous treatises signed during the French Wars of Religion and culminating in the Edict of Nantes (1598), granting French Huguenots limited rights of worship, are prime examples of this tactical use of toleration. Concluding that in the period religious tolerance was 'a kind of charitable hatred', Walsham observes that 'toleration was a paradoxical policy, a casuistical stance involving a deliberate suspension of righteous hostility and, consequently, a considerable degree of moral discomfort. From the outside looking in, it might look very much like apathy, cowardice and a contemptibly lax and lukewarm commitment to upholding the true religion' (4). If, as Thomas Scanlon asserts, 'Widespread acceptance of the idea of religious toleration is, at least in North America and Europe, a historical legacy of the European Wars of Religion' (188), it stands in marked contrast to the dominant thinking about religious difference in the early modern European culture that produced those wars.

Early modern European culture had numerous sexual, cultural, and intellectual bugbears such as sodomy, witchcraft, and atheism. Why would religious tolerance be among them? Certainly, religious tolerance might not seem to belong with other notions to which early modern Europeans were hostile, and certainly early modern Europe had need of such a notion, especially after the Protestant Reformation, as the French Wars of Religion and then the Thirty Years War demonstrate. The difficulty that the idea might have posed to early modern thought emerges, however, when considered in the light of such modern definitions of toleration as Catriona McKinnon's, who writes that 'Toleration is a matter of putting up with that which you oppose: the motto of the tolerant person is "live and let live", even when what she lets live shocks, enrages, frightens, or disgusts her' (3). Toleration tolerates difference *as difference*, without seeking to efface it. In contrast, as Walsham observes in relation to early modern England,

> In a context in which truth was held to be single and indivisible, the persecution of dissident minorities was logical, rational and legitimate. Ecclesiastical and secular authorities were believed to have a solemn responsibility to punish those who departed from orthodoxy, to use any means necessary to uphold the true religion and reclaim those who strayed from the straight and narrow way. (1)

Religious tolerance, moreover, was a difficult and potentially dangerous idea, because to countenance it, in its radical form at least, would be to call into question the foundations of dominant early modern conceptualisations of political power, which conflated political and religious unity and authority. Jean Bodin, whom Skinner describes as a 'moderate Catholic' (253), argues in his *Six*

Books of a Commonweal (1576) that 'seeing that disputations of religion bring not only the doubt and overthrow of religions, but even the ruin and destruction of commonweals also, it behooveth them to be by most strait laws forbidden' (Bodin, 537). Conversely, Bodin asserts

> That there is nothing which doth more uphold and maintain the estates and commonweals than religion, and that it is the principal foundation of the power and strength of monarchies and seignories, as also for the execution of justice, for the obedience of the subjects, the reverence of the magistrates, for the fear of doing evil, and for the mutual love and amity of everyone towards other, it is by most strait and severe laws to be provided. (537)

In Elizabethan England, of course, Bodin's position was actual political fact: the Act of Supremacy (1559), the Act of Uniformity (1559), and the Thirty-Nine Articles (1563) conflated religious and political authority in Elizabeth as the 'Supreme Governor of the Church' (Guy, 261) as well as of the state, and made deviation from the ritual and dogmatic uniformity that she had ordained a crime. In 1571 the bishop of London, Edwin Sandys, stated the case succinctly:

> This liberty, that men may openly profess diversity of religion, must needs be dangerous ... One god, one king, one faith, one profession, is fit for one monarchy and commonwealth. Division weakeneth; concord strengtheneth ... Let conformity and unity in religion be provided for; and it shall be as a wall of defence unto this realm. (qtd Walsham, 39–40)

Visible expressions of real religious difference detracted from the power of the sovereign, threatened the stability of the commonwealth, and therefore could not be countenanced. Hence the persecution of the Puritans as well as the Catholics during the latter decades of Elizabeth's reign.

What early modern Europe lacked, then, was a positive conceptualisation of the completely secular state, within which religious differences could coexist tolerantly if not always comfortably. Nonetheless, early modern Europeans had several examples of states in which religious differences were tolerated close at hand, perhaps too close at hand: Poland (of which Anjou becomes king in scene 10 of the play) and the Ottoman Empire. By the seventeenth century, the Ottoman Empire comprised numerous heteroglot regions with several different religions on the three different continents of Europe, Asia, and Africa (Imber, 1–3). Colin Imber writes that

> The population of the Empire was heterogeneous in religion, language, and social structure. As the faith of the sultans and of the ruling élite, Islam was the dominant religion, but the Greek and Armenian Orthodox churches retained an important place within the political structure of the Empire, and ministered to large Christian populations which, in many areas, outnumbered Muslims. There was also a substantial population of Ottoman Jews. (1)

Religious minorities were not persecuted but allowed considerable self-governance, including establishing their own legal systems (Imber, 204–5). Imber notes that 'Muslims alone could achieve political office, but even here Muslim descent was unnecessary. Many, if not most, political office holders were first- or second-generation converts from Christianity' (2). This aspect of their feared neighbour's polity did not pass by early modern European eyes unnoticed and unremarked. Although committed to religious uniformity, Bodin in *Six Books of a Commonweal* still records with 'open admiration' (Goffman, 111) that

> The great Emperor of the Turks doth with as great devotion as any prince in the world honour and observe the religion by him received from his ancestors, and yet detesteth he not the strange religions of others but to the contrary permitteth every man to live according to his conscience. Yea and that more is, near unto his palace at Pera, suffereth four divers religions, *viz.* that of the Jews, that of the Christians, that of the Grecians, and that of the Mahometans; and besides that, sendeth alms unto the Calogers or religious monks dwelling upon the mountain Athos (being Christians) to pray for him. (Bodin, 538)

Significantly, by 1597 early modern Londoners would have access to another example of Eastern religious tolerance: Tamburlaine. Published in French in 1595 and in English translation in 1597, Jean Dubec-Crespin's *The History of the Great Emperor Tamerlan* presents the conqueror as a figure of remarkable religious tolerance. In Dubec-Crespin's account, Tamburlaine himself is a religious eclectic, and his right-hand man Axalla is Christian. When asked why 'he did not constrain with the sword all religions to embrace his', Tamburlaine replies, 'I will never do it. For I cannot believe but God is delighted with the diversity of religion ... This is the cause wherefore I suffer within my dominions everyone to worship God in any manner whatsoever' (Dubec-Crespin, 298).

The Massacre at Paris does not mention Tamburlaine at all and only once refers to the Ottoman Empire. Poland, Anjou tells the ambassadors who have come to offer him the Polish crown in scene 10, is 'worthy such a king' (5) as is able to conduct 'The greatest wars within our Christian bounds, / I mean our wars against the Muscovites / And, on the other side, against the Turk' (10–12). Anjou was offered the crown in June 1573. Poland was an elective monarchy, and according to Anjou what the Polish voters were looking for when they elected him king, against stiff competition from such figures as Maximillian the Holy Roman Emperor, was a leader 'whom practice long hath taught / To please himself with manage of the wars' (8–9). This may be so, but historically the Poles had something else on their minds as well in the wake of the Paris massacres, which had occurred in the middle of Anjou's campaign for the Polish crown (a campaign organised largely by Catherine): religious toleration. One of the terms of Anjou's election was a promise to respect Poland's long tradition of religious toleration, newly enshrined in the Warsaw Confederation (1573) (Jouanna, 169). The play does not register this significant historical fact. Rather, it places Anjou's assumption of the Polish crown in the context of the ongoing pursuit of military conflict based on religious difference: the united Catholics against the Eastern Orthodox Russians ('Muscovites') and the Islamic Ottoman Empire ('the Turk'). Western Europe's two geopolitically prominent examples of institutionalised religious toleration are here reframed as peripheral participants in an international network of violence motivated by religious intolerance. Not surprisingly, Anjou's sojourn on these peripheries is brief (historically, Anjou lasted about four months in Poland before running away), and by scene 14 he has returned to the centre of the action: a France still torn apart by religious warfare.

It is instructive to compare the opening of The Massacre at Paris to the opening of 2 Tamburlaine, a play in which Marlowe very explicitly considers the possibility of radical religious toleration at the political level. 2 Tamburlaine opens with the signing of a truce between Orcanes, king of Natolia and provisional leader of the Turks, and Sigismond, king of Hungary and leader of the European military coalition. The conflict between the two groups is framed in explicitly religious terms: 'shall we parley with the Christian',

Orcanes asks his advisors, 'Or cross the stream and meet him in the field?' (11–12). Both sides opt for a truce and, remarkably, ratify it on the basis of the recognition of religious difference *as difference*. Sigismond swears by 'The Son of God' (1.1.134) to 'keep this peace inviolable' (136), while Orcanes vows 'to keep this truce inviolable' (142) 'By sacred Mahomet, the friend of God, / Whose holy Alcoran remains with us' (137–8). Unlike the letters exchanged between the Ottoman Emperor Murad III and Queen Elizabeth in 1579–80, which sought to find religious common ground by invoking a God 'who only is above all things and all men, and is a most severe revenger of all idolatry, and is jealous of his honour against the false gods of the nations' ('The answer', 243), the oaths of Orcanes and Sigismond highlight the differences between Islam and Christianity. An early modern Christian would be unlikely to concede either that Mahomet was God's friend or that the Qur'an was a sacred text, while Islam explicitly rejects the idea that Jesus is the divine Son of God, however much it might honour Jesus as a prophet. In the opening scene of *2 Tamburlaine*, then, the recognition and toleration of religious difference is made the basis for the real political action of an international peace treaty that is intended to halt the atrocities of war. The moment does not last. Sigismond's advisors remind him of the 'cruel slaughter of our Christian bloods / These heathenish Turks and pagans lately made' (2.1.5–6), assure him that it is not morally wrong to break his oath to 'such infidels, / In whom no faith or true religion rests' (33–4), and threaten that he will suffer 'the vengeance of the Highest' (56) should he 'not kill and curse at God's command' (55). Sigismond then orders the recommencement of religious war: 'Then arm, my lords, and issue suddenly, / Giving commandment to our general host / With expedition to assail the pagan / And take the victory our God hath given' (59–62). Sigismond's ambush attack fails, but the play does not further countenance the idea of the toleration of religious difference as difference. Rather, as Tamburlaine burns the Qur'an at the end of the play, he declares to his soldiers that 'Mahomet remains in hell' (5.2.134) and urges them to 'Seek out another godhead to adore, / The God that sits in heaven, if any God, / For he is God alone, and none but he' (136–8). To establish a new God, no matter how abstract and all-encompassing, requires sending the old ones to hell first; the new God claims exclusive rights to human worship, just as did the ones that he displaced. The religious toleration dramatised in the play's opening scene is here at its conclusion emphatically rejected; the endless pursuit of the true God expresses itself as relentless religious war.

Like *2 Tamburlaine*, *The Massacre at Paris* opens with a moment of religious toleration that subsequently falls apart. The wedding ceremony in the play's first scene is visibly not a blending of Protestant and Catholic ritual from which all traces of religious differences have been erased. Charles is the scene's mediating figure, and he expresses the 'wish' that 'this union and religious league, / Knit in these hands thus joined in nuptial rites, / May not dissolve till death dissolve our lives' (3–5). Like Orcanes, the mediating Turk in *2 Tamburlaine*, Charles seeks to bring about peace by establishing a political relationship, a 'league', between two warring factions. Like the oaths sworn by Orcanes and Sigismond, however, the 'nuptial rites' by which the league will be established acknowledge rather than efface religious difference. '[T]he marriage rites performed' (18), Charles tells his mixed religious company, 'We think it good to go and consummate / The rest with hearing of a holy mass' (19–20), but 'The rest that will not go, my lords, may stay' (23). The royal wedding moves forward towards its goal of establishing peace and unity by tolerating religious difference as difference. The radical nature of this approach to religious toleration is signalled by the amount of immediate opposition it garners from Catholic and Protestant sides alike. If, as has been mentioned, the play makes Catherine the voice of the Catholic opposition, the Protestants who remain on stage after the Catholic characters have exited into the church are no less bigoted in their religious rhetoric. To conclude the scene, Navarre prays that 'God may still defend the right of France' (55), which he equates with the propagation of Protestantism, 'mak[ing] His Gospel flourish in this land' (56).

Under the pressure of this opposition, the moment of radical religious toleration instantiated by the wedding proves to be as ephemeral as the league between the Christians and the Ottomans in *2 Tamburlaine*. After the assassination of Navarre's mother and the attempted assassination of the Admiral, the two sides retreat into religiously motivated conflict in which the rhetoric of intolerance proves to be the most persuasive to those involved. Scene 4, the council scene, provides a prime example. Catherine begins the discussion by figuring the Protestants as 'the fatal straggling deer' (2) who are now trapped 'Within the compass of a deadly toil' (3) and must be hunted and killed while the opportunity lasts. Anjou follows this up by advising the King that 'the wisest note their proper griefs / And rather seek to scourge their enemies / Than be themselves base subjects to the whip' (14–16), further entrenching the us-and-them divide between Protestants and Catholics within the logic of a conflict that admits of no toleration or compromise. Guise then echoes Anjou's argument and urges Charles 'to seek your country's good' (19) rather than 'pity or relieve these upstart heretics' (20), rhetorically undoing the unity Charles proclaimed in scene 1 and positing a different kind of national unity based on the expulsion of religious difference, the elimination of 'upstart heretics'. Charles's intervention in the discussion is consistent with his position in the opening scene but is weak. The Protestants 'justly challenge their protection' (8) because they have been given the 'safety of our word' (7) and are '[o]nly corrupted in religion' (10). For Charles, monarchical authority transcends religious difference and mandates that religious difference should be tolerated. The word 'corrupted', however, suggests that even Charles has difficulty conceiving of religious difference as legitimate, and he abandons his defence of toleration immediately after Catherine concludes this deliberative part of the discussion by declaring, 'I hope these reasons may serve my princely son / To have some care for fear of enemies' (21–2). That 'care', of course, takes shape next morning as the St Bartholomew's Day massacres.

With Charles's acquiescence to his council's arguments in scene 4, the play abandons the idea of the toleration of religious difference as difference. Potential mediating figures such as Charles, Taleus, and Ramus die, flee, or are murdered. The rhetoric of religious intolerance dominates the major characters' speeches, from Navarre, who in scene 16 vows to fight to defend 'our true religion' (6), and Guise, whose dying declaration is '*Vive la messe!* Perish Huguenots' (21.82), to Catherine, who upon the news of Guise's murder laments, 'The Protestants will glory and insult, / Wicked Navarre will get the crown of France, / The Popedom cannot stand, all goes to wrack' (21.152–4). The play intermittently attempts to defuse the rhetoric of religious intolerance by transposing it into dynastic conflict or the Machiavellian pursuit of power. A conspicuous example of the former is the Cardinal's statement to Catherine in scene 14 that his brother 'hath gathered a power of men, / Which, as he saith, to kill the Puritans, / But 'tis the house of Bourbon that he means' (54–6). Guise himself provides a blatant example of the latter in his extended soliloquy in scene 2, informing the audience that 'My policy hath framed religion' (64) and that 'I am ashamed, however that I seem, / To think a word of such a simple sound / Of so great matter should be made the ground' (66–8). Religious intolerance escapes these attempts at confinement, however. In Catherine's lament over Guise, for example, dynastic conflict is clearly of secondary importance to her religious concerns, and Guise's cool Machiavellian rhetoric in scene 2 cannot mask the murderous religious zealotry he displays throughout the play, whether in the massacre scenes or in his dying words.

More effectively, the play's characters sometimes attempt to convert the religious issue into one of national sovereignty and unity. In scene 16 Navarre vows to 'fight / In honour of our God and country's good' (10–11) as well as in defence of 'our true religion' (6), for example, and in scene 18 he declares that he will 'beat the papal monarch from our lands / And keep those relics from our countries' coasts' (16–17). One of Henry III's chief complaints against Guise displays the same strategy: 'Hath he not made me in the Pope's defence / To spend the treasure that should strength my land / In civil broils between Navarre and me' (21.103–5). Religious differences are here minimised in relation to the financial and national turmoil created by conflict described as 'civil broils'. This strategy permits the reconciliation between the two Henrys in the concluding scene. Even so, it does not eliminate the rhetoric of religious intolerance. As he dies from his knife wound, Henry exhorts Épernon to 'whet thy sword on Sixtus' bones, / That it may keenly slice the Catholics' (24.99–100) and declares himself now to be the 'faithful friend' (24.106) of the Protestant 'Queen of England' (24.105). After Henry's death, Navarre continues Henry's rhetoric, concluding the play by vowing that 'Rome and all those popish prelates there / Shall curse the time that e'er Navarre was King / And ruled in France by Henry's fatal death' (24.110–12). Having begun with the prospect of national unity based on the toleration of religious difference as difference, the play concludes with the violent assertion of national unity based on religious intolerance. If the latter is measured against the former – and the central presence of Navarre at both ends of this trajectory from wedding to funeral might encourage us to do so – the critical rather than propagandistic nature of the play's dark vision becomes apparent. Religious intolerance leads only to further conflict; even though it fails from the start in the play, the toleration of religious difference as difference is the

INTRODUCTION 39

only means to halt the repetition of atrocities committed in the name of God.

PERFORMANCE HISTORY

The Massacre at Paris was written between 1589, the date of Henry III's assassination, and 1593, when theatre owner and company manager Philip Henslowe recorded in his diary the taking of three pounds and fourteen shillings for the performance on 30 January by Lord Strange's Men (Manley and MacLean, 88) at the Rose Theatre of 'the tragedy of the gvyes' (Foakes, 20), which he marks as 'ne' or new. The Rose was an open-air amphitheatre built in 1587 in the southern London suburb of Southwark on the site of a rose garden. Initially, it might have doubled as a bear-baiting pit and might have had a removable stage (Greenfield and Gurr, 336–7), but in 1592 its owner, Henslowe, renovated its stage and expanded its seating capacity (Gurr, *Shakespeare's Opposites*, 125). Even after the renovations, the Rose and its stage remained small in comparison to other open-air amphitheatres of the period: in contrast to the Globe's roughly forty by thirty feet dimensions (Gurr, *Shakespearean Stage*, 146), Andrew Gurr describes the Rose's stage as 'a hexagon of less than thirty-five feet wide with a depth of less than half that' (*Shakespeare's Opposites*, 132), which was not 'much more than five hundred feet of floor space, markedly smaller than any calculated for other stages of the time' (127). Nonetheless, on this new stage the sum taken for Marlowe's new play was the largest Henslowe records for the 1592/3 season. In 1594, when the London theatres reopened after having been closed because of the plague, the play had a run of ten performances by Henslowe's company, the Lord Admiral's Men, being staged on 19 and 25 June, 3, 8, 16 and 27 July, 8 and 17 August, and 7 and 25 September. During this period from June to the end of September, *The Massacre at Paris* shared the stage with three other Marlowe plays: *The Jew of Malta* (seven performances), *Tamburlaine* (three performances), and *Doctor Faustus* (one performance) (Foakes, 22–4). The play was revived in November 1598, when Henslowe lent William Borne money 'to buy a pair of silk stockings to play the Guise in' (Foakes, 76) and 'to embroider his hat for the Guise' (Foakes, 82). Between 3 and 26 November 1601, Henslowe spent seven pounds, fourteen shillings and sixpence on costumes for a further revival of the play (Foakes, 183–5), which might have been performed at

Henslowe's new open-air amphitheatre the Fortune, which had a much larger, rectangular stage forty-three feet wide and twenty-seven-and-a-half feet deep (Gurr, *Shakespeare's Opposites*, 138). Given his fame for performing the star roles in Marlowe's plays and the fact that a 1602 inventory of his wardrobe contains items for 'the Guises' (Foakes, 293), it is highly likely that Henslowe's celebrity-actor son-in-law Edward Alleyn performed the role of the Guise in 1594. William Borne seems to have been given the role in 1598, when Alleyn retired from the stage, and William Jube in 1601. The references to the 1601 costume expenses are the last indications Henslowe's diary provides of the play's early modern performance.

However small the Rose stage may have been in comparison to other playhouses, *The Massacre at Paris* made full and imaginative use of it. As well as a balcony area 'above', the tiring house façade of the Rose stage had two side doors and a set of main doors in the centre. Theatre historian Andrew Gurr states that its 'main entry-point was the middle one of the three, sometimes now called the "discovery space", a broad opening with most likely a pair of doors' (*Shakespeare's Opposites*, 124). According to Gurr, the discovery space 'probably made a third entry-point' (*Shakespearean Stage*, 151) on to the main stage for actors, the other two being the main tiring house façade doors and the trap door to allow actors to enter from below the stage. The 'discovery space' or 'inner stage' could have been used to represent a variety of spaces, such as a study, as at the beginning of scene 9 of the play, or an inner chamber, as in scene 21. Gurr cites instances from Barnaby Barnes's *The Devil's Charter* in which

> the leading character enters '*out of his studie*', and later exits '*into his studie*', which we might suppose to be through one of the normal entry doors if it were not that in two other scenes he is discovered in his study and speaks six or eight lines there before moving out onto the stage. (*Shakespearean Stage*, 151)

Marlowe's *Doctor Faustus*, initially performed at the Rose, opens with '*Enter* Faustus *in his study*' (1.1.0 SD) and places Faustus in this space on several subsequent occasions. Dessen and Thomson cite numerous instances of characters entering from the discovery space (69–70). Given that audience sight lines would be limited, however, presumably the dramatic action would move on to the main staging area fairly quickly.

Scene 21 of the play, in which Guise is assassinated, provides a prime example of the versatility and fluidity of the playhouse stage. The scene requires (at least) three 'locations': Henry's 'royal cabinet' or private chamber, an ante-chamber space immediately outside the private chamber, and the 'next room' in which the assassins conceal themselves. As do scenes 5 and 9, the scene illustrates the way in which the Elizabethan stage could be 'split' to represent multiple locales. The scene's characters enter and exit these locations rapidly, without the play's stage directions giving any clear indication of where exactly on the stage the characters are moving from and to. In the first 26 lines, for example, the octavo provides stage directions for three entrances: the Captain and the Murderers, followed by Henry and Épernon, then Guise. No exit directions are given, but the dialogue indicates that at some point the Captain, the Murderers, Henry, and (arguably) Épernon all must exit. The Murderers must conceal themselves, and Henry and Épernon must retreat into Henry's private chamber. Where the Murderers hide and what stage space is chosen to represent the private chamber will determine the point from which Guise then enters the stage, which then will determine the blocking for the rest of the scene's action. The flexibility of the playhouse stage and the absence of explicit stage directions create multiple staging possibilities for the flow of action in the opening sequence of this scene. Obviously, the actors in the Admiral's Men would have blocked the movement out with some precision. Modern readers and directors are left to their own conjectural devices, limited only by the knowledge of the playing spaces available and by their own imaginative interpretations of the stage action implied by the dialogue and the minimal stage directions. This editor has made his own conjectural reconstruction of the stage action of the scene, explained in the commentary notes, but it should be emphasised that it represents only a possibility, not a certainty.

After 1601 we have no record of a performance of *The Massacre at Paris* until 1940, when the Yale Dramatic Association performed the play, directed by Burton G. Shevelove. The play was performed at least five more times in the twentieth century: on 30 January 1963 by the Marlowe Society at the Chanticleer Theatre in London; in 1981 by the Glasgow Citizens' Theatre; in 1985 by the Royal Shakespeare Company; and in 1998, in Paris and New York, in Roman Paska's adapted version, *Dieu!: God Mother Radio* (Esche, 316; Cahill, 169).

The 1981 Glasgow Citizens' Theatre production demonstrated the potential of Marlowe's play on the modern stage. The production was directed by Philip Prowse and performed by seven actors. Though the dialogue was not cut, no attempt was made to reconstruct original staging conditions, and the character of Queen Elizabeth was added to the play as an onstage figure observing and presiding over the action (much like Don Andrea and Revenge in *The Spanish Tragedy*). The overwhelming impression given by reviewers is that the production's goal was maximum *visual* impact. Reviewing for the *Glasgow Herald*, Mary Brennan describes the actors as 'A band of sixteenth-century players' in 'lead-white faces, sumptuous black costumes'. Ned Chaillet, reviewing for *The Times*, noted that 'the small cast is multiplied by cheap dummies, which serve as plentiful corpses', a strategy that the Admiral's Men might have employed as well with its staging of the Lord Admiral's death in scene 5 and the subsequent treatment of his body. According to the *Financial Times*'s Michael Coveney, 'The stage, rising by steps from the auditorium, [was] like some Gothic altar prepared for a funeral. Bunches of candles illumine[d] the black-draped edifice.' Two traverse curtains at the back of the stage served as the changing room and tiring house façade. The play was 'a whirl of black and gold'. Not all reviewers were equally enthused by the production's spectacularly visual nature: the *Guardian*'s Corelia Oliver, for example, dismissed the play as 'an empty, ranting piece full of cardboard characters, in which spectacle is not enough to alleviate boredom'; the play 'ought to have remained in the library'. The consensus, however, seems to have been that the *visual* spectacle of the play *was* enough to alleviate the supposed *textual* defects that have often led editors to consign it to the library as, in *TLS* reviewer W. W. Robson's words, a 'pot-boiler, rapidly and carelessly thrown together'.

Paska's 1998 production further developed the performative potential of Marlowe's pot-boiler. Patricia Cahill writes that Paska's adaptation 'appropriated Marlowe's urgent, journalistic style' and 'embraced the self-conscious extravagance of camp. Combining docu-journalism with ludicrous implausibility, *Dieu* featured Massimo Schuster as a garrulous talk-radio host who punctuated his reports on the killing with loud music selections' (Cahill, 156). The performance was made even more striking by the fact that 'the supporting cast consisted not of actors but of marionettes, which Schuster, a renowned European puppeteer, operated in full view of the audience. Miming brutality, he grabbed these gorgeous wooden figures from onstage racks, flung them about, and abruptly tossed them aside' (156). The play, Cahill argues, created

> a distinctive kind of affect I call the *feeling of reenactment*, that is, the peculiar feeling that you are really 'there', plunged into the past. What *Dieu* emphasizes through torture-porn thrills and time-travel clichés is that the restaging of history entails much more than an invitation to ponder the past. *Massacre* summons playgoers to *feel* this history impinging upon the present. (157)

Indeed, in the first two decades of the twenty-first century, *The Massacre at Paris* has demonstrated considerable power to impinge upon the present, with seven productions of which I am aware between 2000 and 2018. The play was directed by Alex Johnston and performed by the Bedrock Theatre company in Dublin in 2002. There were three productions in 2014 as part of celebrations of Marlowe's 450th birthday: two student productions, one in Cambridge and another at the Canterbury Cathedral Crypt, and the Dolphin's Back production of the play at the Rose in London, directed by James Wallace. Steve Orman reviewed the Dolphin's Back production for *Early Modern Literary Studies*. The production, he writes, was 'full of dark humour' but 'incredibly beautiful on an artistic level' and was 'successful in perfectly blending the macabre and the humorous' (1–2). In March 2018, the play was performed again in Cambridge, at Christ's College Chapel, directed by Thomas Dixon.

The play's recent popularity has extended beyond the British Isles. Paska's adaptation is a late twentieth-century example, and there have been three French productions in the opening two decades of the twenty-first. The Compagnie X ici performed the play at the Théatre National de Toulouse in March 2007 and the Théatre National de Strasboug in January 2008, directed by Guillaume Delaveau. In the *Shakespeare Bulletin*, reviewer Nathalie Rivere de Carles writes of the Toulouse performance that

> From the very first moments of the performance, the spectators were trapped in a temporal net designed by the scenographer and the director. The wide proscenium arch stage of the Theatre de Toulouse was scattered with a puzzling combination of props: stage left, a skeleton was cycling on a bike actuating a grindstone. A breastplate and a sword could be seen on the floor near that ominous machine. Stage right, one could see a piano on a gyrating platform. The contrast between both devices set the tone

of the production. Delaveau's *Massacre at Paris* was to be a fascinating dance of death for all times. (144)

According to Rivere de Carles, Delaveau 'insisted on the incomplete nature of the Marlovian script and took the decision to fill the textual blanks with different temporal landmarks. The result was a breathless, visually violent production that played with the audience's historical and theatrical frames of reference' (143). The play was produced in equally stunning fashion in 2016 by Théâtre 2 l'Acte at the Théatre du Ring in Toulouse, directed by Marie-Angèle Vaurs. Reviewer Serge Pey writes that the production 'crève nos yeux sonores dans une actualité terrible au Moyen-Orient, en France et dans le monde. Au nom du religieux les monstruosités se succèdent a l'infini. Les définitions de Dieu se cachent dans les contexts de géostratégie, de guerre pétrolière ou d'oppression traditionelle patriarcale' ['makes plain to us a terrible reality in the Middle East, in France, and throughout the world. In the name of religion, one monstrosity succeeds another *ad infinitum*. Definitions of God lurk as much behind geostrategy and petroleum wars as behind traditional patriarchal oppression'] (Pey, 4). What the recent production history of Marlowe's least-respected play emphatically demonstrates, then, is that in the hands of directors and theatre companies willing to understand and work with the play's alternative traumatic aesthetics, it can be a disturbingly powerful and moving work of art that speaks loudly, if not always eloquently, to the present.

THE TEXT

In addition to the performance-related entries cited in the previous section, Henslowe's diary also records that on 18 January 1602 he paid Alleyn six pounds for three playbooks: *The French Doctor*, *The Massacre at Paris*, and *The Nut* (Foakes, 187). *The Massacre at Paris* was not, however, entered in the Stationers' Register before its publication in octavo format sometime before 1602 or 1603, when, according to Robert Welsh, 'the head-piece which appears on A3 of the octavo was badly damaged on its lower right side' (qtd Esche, 295). The play collates A–D8. A1 and D7^r–D8^v are blank, and the play begins on A3, with the undamaged head-piece. The title page of the play, A2^r, states that the play was printed by E.A. [Edward Allde] for Edward White but bears no date. The last Revels editor of the play, H. J. Oliver, contends that 'On the whole, the most probable date of publication is 1602 – perhaps shortly after Henslowe's company purchased the authentic text from Alleyn' (xlviii–xlix). The editor of the recent Oxford old-spelling edition, Edward J. Esche, argues for the much earlier date of 1593 or 1594 on the basis of typographical and compositorial evidence first presented by Welsh that suggests that the same compositor or compositors set *The Massacre at Paris* and Thomas Kyd's *The Spanish Tragedy*, also published in an undated octavo but, in Esche's words, 'confidently thought to be 1592' (295). In 2011, R. Carter Hailey proposed the date of 1596, basing his conclusion on the match between the paper on which the octavo was printed and the paper of John Harington's *Metamorphosis of Ajax*, printed in 1596, also in octavo format (Hailey, 32–3). Although the arguments for none of these dates are absolutely conclusive and the dating of the play must remain inexact, the weight of the evidence strongly suggests that the octavo was printed in 1596.

If *The Massacre at Paris* was reprinted in the early modern period, no copy of the reprint has survived. The play was next reprinted in editions by Oxberry (1818) and Broughton (1818). As well as being included in the numerous nineteenth- and twentieth-century editions of Marlowe's complete works, the play has also been published as the second play in several two-play editions, the most significant of which are H. S. Bennett's *'The Jew of Malta' and 'The Massacre at Paris'* (London, 1931), H. J. Oliver's Revels edition, *'Dido Queen of Carthage' and 'The Massacre at Paris'* (Cambridge, MA, 1968), and Edward J. Esche's edition of the play in volume five of the Oxford *Complete Works of Christopher Marlowe* (Oxford, 1998), which also includes both parts of *Tamburlaine*. The only twentieth-century single-play edition of *The Massacre at Paris* is W. W. Greg's Malone Society Reprint edition (1929 [1928]).

The octavo has often been suspected of being a 'bad quarto', a memorial reconstruction, because of its brevity, its repetitiveness, its irregular poetry, and its numerous echoes of Marlowe's own *Edward II* and Shakespeare's *2* and *3 Henry VI*. The notion of the 'bad quarto', developed by the New Bibliography in the first half of the twentieth century, has come under attack in recent editorial theory, most notably by Laurie Maguire in *Shakespearean Suspect Texts: The 'Bad' Quartos and their Contexts*. Of the 41 playtexts conventionally considered to be bad quartos, Maguire contends, only four contain strong evidence of memorial reconstruction. Significantly, *The Massacre at Paris* is one of those texts (Maguire, 324). The case for the surviving text of the play being a distorted or condensed version of a fuller version is strengthened by the existence of what is known as the 'Collier Leaf', discovered by J. P. Collier in 1825 and now in the Folger Library (MS J.b.8). A modernised version of the Collier leaf has been included in an appendix to this edition. The manuscript leaf provides a fuller, slightly less garbled, verse version of the first sixteen lines of scene 19 of the play. Maguire's analysis of the document concludes that it is not a Collier forgery: Collier 'was simply not capable of this standard of paleographical forgery in the 1820s and 1830s (when he announced the discovery of the leaf)' (Maguire, 324). Building on R. E. Alton's comparison of the handwriting of the leaf and Marlowe's signature, Esche contends that the leaf is not a holograph but rather 'a scribal copy of an unknown original' (298). The provenance of the leaf and its authority remain debatable, however, and the editor of the play is left with the octavo as the sole copy text for a modern edition of the play, despite its putatively corrupt state.

The octavo poses few specific editorial difficulties, and I have confined emendation to the necessary minimum, documented in the collation notes. Ten witnesses of the octavo survive, housed in the following institutions: the British Library; the Bodleian Library; the Pepys Library, Magdalene College, Cambridge; the Parker Library, Corpus Christi College, Cambridge; the Victoria and Albert Museum; the Library of Congress; the Folger Library; the Huntington Library; the Newberry Library; and the Chapin Library, Williams College, Massachusetts. My collation of all ten copies discovered four stop-press textual variants, recorded in the collation notes.

The octavo contains no act or scene divisions. This edition follows Bullen's (1885) division of the play into 24 scenes. To indicate their editorial provenance, the scene divisions, along with additions to stage directions (which, as this introduction has already indicated, are often inexact), have been placed in square brackets in the text. Speech prefixes abbreviated in the octavo have been silently expanded in the text but modernised. The octavo's spelling and punctuation have also been silently modernised, as have the play's character and place names. The major characters' first names have also been Anglicised: Henry instead of Henri, for example. Early modern texts quoted in this introduction and the commentary notes have been silently modernised as well. References to Shakespeare are to the seventh edition of David Bevington's *The*

Complete Works of Shakespeare, although, when citing parallel passages between *The Massacre at Paris* and *The Second Part of Henry VI* and *The Third Part of Henry VI,* I have quoted the 1594 and 1595 editions (*The First Part of the Contention* and *The True Tragedy*) respectively in an attempt to return more closely to what was current in the theatre in the 1590s than might be reflected in the revised versions of these two plays published in the 1623 Folio.

THE MASSACRE AT PARIS, WITH THE DEATH OF THE DUKE OF GUISE

[List of characters, in order of appearance:

CHARLES IX, *King of France.*
CATHERINE, *Catherine de Medici, Queen Mother of France.*
NAVARRE, *Henry Bourbon, King of Navarre and later Henry IV, King of France.*
CONDÉ, *Navarre's cousin.* 5
LORD ADMIRAL, *Gaspard de Coligny, Seigneur de Châtillon.*
MARGARET, *Marguerite de Valois, Charles's sister.*
GUISE, *Henry, Duke of Guise.*
QUEEN NAVARRE, *Jeanne d'Albret, Navarre's mother.*
ANJOU, *Henry de Valois, Charles's brother and later Henry III,* 10
King of France.
DUMAINE, *Charles, Duke of Mayenne, Guise's brother.*
COSSEINS, *Captain of Charles's royal guard.*
GONZAGUE, *Duke of Nevers.*
RETZ, *a Count.* 15
MONTSOREAU, *a Count.*
LÉRAN, *a Huguenot preacher.*
SEROUNE, *a Huguenot.*
SEROUNE'S Wife
RAMUS, *Pierre de la Ramée, a philosophy professor at the* 20
Collège Royal.
TALEUS, *Ramus's friend.*
CARDINAL OF LORRAINE, *Louis, Cardinal of Guise, Guise's brother.*
ÉPERNON, *Jean-Louis de la Valette, Henry III's chief minion.* 25
PLESSIS, *Philippe de Mornay, Seigneur de Plessis Marly, Navarre's advisor.*
MAUGIRON, *Louis de Maugiron, one of Henry III's mignons and the Duchess of Guise's lover.*
DUCHESS OF GUISE, *Catherine de Clèves, Countess of Eu.* 30
BARTAS, *Guillaume de Salluste, Seigneur du Bartas, Navarre's advisor.*
JOYEUSE, *Anne de Joyeuse, one of Henry's chief mignons.*

Heading List of Characters ... murderers] *this edn; not in O.*

50

SC. 1]   THE MASSACRE AT PARIS   51

YOUNG GUISE, *Charles de Lorraine, Guise's son.*
Apothecary   35
Lords of Poland
Cutpurse
Duchess of Guise's Maid
Captain of Henry III's Guard
Friar   40
Surgeon
English Agent
Soldiers, Messengers, Attendants, Commoners, Huguenots,
    Schoolmasters, and Murderers]

[SCENE 1]

Enter CHARLES *the French King, the* QUEEN MOTHER
[CATHERINE], *the King of* NAVARRE, *the Prince of*
CONDÉ, *the* LORD HIGH ADMIRAL, *and the Queen of*
Navarre [MARGARET], *with others.*

Charles. Prince of Navarre my honourable brother,
    Prince Condé, and my good Lord Admiral,
    I wish this union and religious league,
    Knit in these hands thus joined in nuptial rites,

Heading Sc. 1.] Bullen (subst); not in O. 0.2. SD. CONDÉ] O *(*Condye*).*
Modernised silently throughout. 2. Condé] O *(*Condy*). Modernised silently*
throughout.

   [The play's opening scene takes place on 18 August 1572 outside
Notre-Dame Cathedral in Paris, immediately after the royal wedding ceremony of Henry Navarre and Margaret Valois (Garrisson, *La Saint-Barthélemy*,
72). According to Hotman, the ceremony used 'a certain form of words, so
framed as disagreed with the religion of neither side' (*True and Plain Report*,
xxxvi).]
   1. SH. Charles] Charles IX, King of France (r. 1560–74).
   1. *Prince of Navarre*] Henry, King of Navarre (r. 1572–1610) and future
Henry IV, King of France (r. 1589–1610).
     brother] i.e. brother-in-law.
   2. *Prince Condé*] Henry de Bourbon-Condé (1552–88), Navarre's cousin.
     Lord Admiral] Gaspard de Coligny (1519–72), Seigneur de Châtillon.
Coligny was Admiral of France 1552–72.
   3. *this ... league*] i.e. this sacred concord between the French Protestants
(Huguenots) and Catholics.
   4. *nuptial*] marriage.

52   THE MASSACRE AT PARIS   [SC. I

  May not dissolve till death dissolve our lives,   5
  And that the native sparks of princely love
  That kindled first this motion in our hearts
  May still be fuelled in our progeny.
Navarre. The many favours which Your Grace hath shown
  From time to time, but specially in this,   10
  Shall bind me ever to Your Highness' will
  In what Queen Mother or Your Grace commands.
Catherine. Thanks, son Navarre. You see we love you well
  That link you in marriage with our daughter here,
  And, as you know, our difference in religion   15
  Might be a means to cross you in your love.
Charles. Well, madam, let that rest.
  And now, my lords, the marriage rites performed,
  We think it good to go and consummate
  The rest with hearing of a holy mass.   20
  Sister, I think yourself will bear us company.
Margaret. I will, my good lord.

---

9. SH. *Navarre.*] *Ribner (subst); Nauar. O.*   13. SH. *Catherine.*] *Ribner (subst); Old Qu. O.*   19–21. consummate / The ... mass. / Sister ... company.] *Broughton (subst);* consumate the rest, / With ... company. *O.*   22. SH. *Margaret.*] *Ribner (subst); Q. Mar. O.*

---

 6. *native*] natural, innate (*OED*, adj., 1a).
 7. *this motion*] i.e. this desire to reconcile France's warring religious factions through the marriage of the Protestant Henry and the Catholic Margaret. See note to lines 49–50.
 8. *fuelled*] given fuel, fed, maintained.
 progeny] children, offspring, descendants.
 9. *Your Grace*] Charles IX.
 11. *Your Highness'*] Charles's.
 12. *Queen Mother*] Catherine de Medici (1519–89), Charles IX's mother.
 14. *daughter*] Margaret de Valois (1553–1615).
 16. *cross*] thwart, oppose, debar (*OED*, v., 14a, b).
 19. *consummate*] complete, finish, put an end to (*OED*, v., 2a, b) but also complete by the act of sexual intercourse (*OED*, v., 1a), thus adumbrating the royal couple's wedding night.

SC. I]   THE MASSACRE AT PARIS   53

Charles. The rest that will not go, my lords, may stay.
   Come, mother, let us go to honour this solemnity.
Catherine. Which I'll dissolve with blood and cruelty.   25
   Exit the King [CHARLES], QUEEN MOTHER [CATHERINE],
         and the Queen of Navarre [MARGARET], *and mane*[n]*t*
                   NAVARRE, *the Prince of* CONDÉ, *and the*
                              LORD HIGH ADMIRAL.
Navarre. Prince Condé and my good Lord Admiral,
   Now Guise may storm but do us little hurt,
   Having the King, Queen Mother on our sides
   To stop the malice of his envious heart
   That seeks to murder all the Protestants.   30
   Have you not heard of late how he decreed,
   If that the King had given consent thereto,
   That all the Protestants that are in Paris
   Should have been murdered the other night?
Admiral. My lord, I marvel that th'aspiring Guise   35
   Dares once adventure without the King's consent
   To meddle or attempt such dangerous things.

---

23. go, my lords, may] *Broughton (subst);* goe (my Lords) may *O.*   25. SH. Catherine.] *Ribner (subst); Old Q. O.*   25.1. SD. QUEEN MOTHER] *Oliver (subst);* Q Mother *O.*   25.2. SD *Queen] Oliver (subst);* Q *O.*   25.1–2 SD.] *centred O.*   26. SH. Navarre.] *Ribner (subst); Nauar. O.*   26. Lord Admiral] *Broughton (subst);* L. Admiral *O.*   28. Queen Mother] *Broughton (subst);* Qu. Mother *O.*   35. SH. Admiral.] *Ribner (subst); Ad. O.*

   23. *stay*] i.e. wait outside the church. Hotman reports that 'the bridegroom, who misliked these ceremonies, together with Henry Prince of Condé, son of Louis, and the Admiral, and other noble men of the same Religion, walked without the church door, waiting for the bride's return' (*True and Plain Report*, xxxviii).
   25.2. SD. *mane*[n] *t*] 'remain' (Latin).
   27. *Guise*] Henry, Duke of Guise (1550–88). Henry became the Duke of Guise in 1563, after his father Francis was assassinated at Orléans during the first War of Religion, which was triggered by Francis's massacre of a group of Huguenots at Vassy in 1562. Gaspard de Coligny was suspected of arranging the assassination (Carroll, 12–20, 166–7).
   storm] rage, protest. Hotman remarks that 'all good men judged the same [the marriage] a most assured pledge and establishment of civil concord, whereas on the contrary part, the Guisians and other enemies of common quietness greatly abhorred the same marriage' (*True and Plain Report*, xxxvi).
   29. *envious*] full of ill-will (*OED*, adj., 2).
   36. *once*] ever, at all, under any circumstances (*OED*, adv., 3a).

Condé. My lord, you need not marvel at the Guise,
    For what he doth the Pope will ratify,
    In murder, mischief, or in tyranny.   40
Navarre. But He that sits and rules above the clouds
    Doth hear and see the prayers of the just
    And will revenge the blood of innocents
    That Guise hath slain by treason of his heart
    And brought by murder to their timeless ends.   45
Admiral. My lord, but did you mark the Cardinal,
    The Guise's brother, and the Duke Dumaine,
    How they did storm at these your nuptial rites
    Because the house of Bourbon now comes in
    And joins your lineage to the crown of France?   50
Navarre. And that's the cause that Guise so frowns at us
    And beats his brains to catch us in his trap,
    Which he hath pitched within his deadly toil.
    Come, my lords, let's go to the church and pray
    That God may still defend the right of France   55
    And make His Gospel flourish in this land.
                                       Exeunt.

---

38. SH. *Condé.*] *Ribner (subst); Con. O.*   38. lord] *Broughton (subst); L. O.*
41. SH. *Navarre.*] *Ribner (subst); Na. O.*   46. SH. *Admiral.*] *Ribner (subst); Ad. O.*   51. SH. *Navarre.*] *Ribner (subst); Na, O.*

---

41. *He*] God.
45. *timeless*] eternal; untimely, premature (*OED*, adj., 1a, 2).
46. *Cardinal*] Historically, Louis, Cardinal of Guise (1555–88), but here confused or conflated with Guise's uncle, Cardinal of Lorraine (1524–74).
47. *Duke Dumaine*] Charles, Duke of Mayenne (1554–1611), also Guise's brother. The octavo's spelling of the Duke's name has been retained in order to preserve the metre.
49–50. *the house ... France*] Henry of Navarre belonged to the French royal house of Bourbon and was next in line to the French crown after Catherine's children, the latest generation of the French royal house of Valois. The marriage between Henry and Margaret joined the houses of Bourbon and Valois and thus had the potential to eliminate dynastic contention between them.
52. *trap*] i.e. plan to 'murder all the Protestants' (30).
53. *toil*] 'a net or nets forming an enclosed area into which a hunted quarry is driven' (*OED*, n.2, 1).

SC. 2] THE MASSACRE AT PARIS 55

[SCENE 2]

Enter the Duke of GUISE.

Guise. If ever Hymen loured at marriage rites
And had his altars decked with dusky lights,
If ever sun stained heaven with bloody clouds
And made it look with terror on the world,
If ever day were turned to ugly night 5
And night made semblance of the hue of hell,
This day, this hour, this fatal night
Shall fully show the fury of them all.
Apothecary.

Enter the Apothecary.

Apothecary. My lord. 10
Guise. Now shall I prove and guerdon to the full
The love thou bearst unto the house of Guise.
Where are those perfumed gloves which I sent

Heading Sc. 2.] *Bullen (subst); not in O.* 9.1. SD. Apothecary] *O (*Pothecarie*). Modernised silently throughout.* 10. SH. *Apothecary.*] *Ribner (subst); Pothe. O.*

[This scene, in which Guise plots the assassination of the Queen of Navarre and the Admiral, is Marlowe's invention. Historically and in Marlowe's sources the Queen died before the wedding, and Guise was not linked to the death (see headnote to scene 3).]

1–2.] Bennett notes that in Book X of *Metamorphoses* Ovid opens his account of the ill-fated marriage of Orpheus to Eurydice by recounting the bad omens that preceded it, among which were that Hymen did not 'sing / The words of that solemnity, nor merry countenance bring, / Nor any handsel of good luck. His torch with drizzling smoke / Was dim' (X.3–6; Bennett, 184).

1. *Hymen*] Greek god of marriage.
loured] frowned, scowled, looked angry (*OED*, v., 1a).
2. *dusky lights*] i.e. dim or smoky candles.
11. *prove*] test.
guerdon] reward.
13. *perfumed gloves*] Hotman claims that the Queen of Navarre 'was poisoned with a venomed smell of a pair of perfumed gloves, dressed by one Renat, the King's apothecary, an Italian' (*True and Plain Report*, xxxv).

        To be poisoned? Hast thou done them? Speak,
        Will every savour breed a pang of death?   15
Apothecary. See where they be, my good lord,
        And he that smells but to them dies.
Guise. Then thou remainest resolute?
Apothecary. I am, my lord, in what Your Grace commands
        till death.
Guise. Thanks, my good friend. I will requite thy love.   20
        Go, then, present them to the Queen Navarre,
        For she is that huge blemish in our eye
        That makes these upstart heresies in France.
        Be gone, my friend. Present them to her straight.
Soldier.   25
                                      Exit Apothecary.

                        Enter a Soldier.

Soldier. My lord.
Guise. Now come thou forth and play thy tragic part.

---

16. SH. *Apothecary.*] Ribner (subst); Pothe. O. 18. resolute?] Broughton (subst); resolute. O. 19. SH. *Apothecary.*] Ribner (subst); Pothe. O. 25.1. SD. Apothecary] Ribner (subst); Pothe O. 26. SH. *Soldier.*] Ribner (subst); Soul. O.

    15.] i.e. will every smell or smelling of the gloves kill?
    17. *but to them*] i.e. merely in their direction.
    20. *requite*] reward, repay.
    21. *Queen Navarre*] Henry of Navarre's mother, Jeanne d'Albret (r. 1555–72).
    22. *blemish in our eye*] an irritant, eyesore, or annoyance. See *The estate of English fugitiues vnder the king of Spaine and his ministers* (1595): 'yet York still remained a blemish in their eye, who always, notwithstanding their base usage, still flourished & bare his head aloft, ranging over the whole country with his Company' (sig. D4').
    23. *makes*] encourages.
    upstart heresies] Protestantism.
    24. *straight*] immediately.
    26. *soldier*] Although Marlowe prefers to keep him anonymous, Hotman identifies the Admiral's assassin as either 'Maurevet, which in the third civil war traitorously slew his captain' or 'Bondot, one of the archers of the King's guard' (*True and Plain Report*, xliii). Modern historians generally agree that the assassin was the former, Charles de Louviers, lord of Maurevet (d. 1583). Maurevet had been raised as a page in the household of Guise's father, and on 22 August 1575 he received from Guise the sizeable sum of 2,000 livres (Carroll, 208–11).

Stand in some window opening near the street,
And when thou seest the Admiral ride by
Discharge thy musket and perform his death, 30
And then I'll guerdon thee with store of crowns.
Soldier. I will, my lord. *Exit* Soldier.
Guise. Now, Guise, begin those deep-engendered thoughts
To burst abroad those never-dying flames
Which cannot be extinguished but by blood. 35
Oft have I levelled and at last have learned
That peril is the chiefest way to happiness
And resolution honour's fairest aim.
What glory is there in a common good
That hangs for every peasant to achieve? 40

---

32. SH. *Soldier.*] *Ribner (subst); Soul. O.* 32. SD. Soldier.] *Ribner (subst); Souldi. O.* 33. begin] *Broughton (subst);* begins *O.*

---

30. *perform*] accomplish, enact; picking up on l.25.

31. *store*] 'sufficient or abundant supply' (*OED*, n., 4a).

crowns] coins.

33. *deep-engendered thoughts*] i.e. thoughts originating deep within Guise's mind and therefore innate or previously concealed.

34. *burst abroad*] OED *burst* cites this example.

34–5. *flames ... blood*] Proverbial: Dent B465.1, 'Only blood can quench the fire'.

36. *levelled*] 'ascertain[ed] the differences of level in (a piece of land)' (*OED*, v.1, 5); *fig.*, surveyed the obstructions preventing me from reaching my goal. Also having the sense of aiming at achieving something, as used by Thomas Wright in his *Passions of the Mind* (1604): 'There can be no man, who works by right reason but ... he aimeth at some end, he levels at some good' (*OED*, v.1, 8a).

37–8.] A version of these lines is included in Robert Allott's *England's Parnassus* (1600): 'Danger's the chiefest joy to happiness, / And resolution honour's fairest aim' (48; Bennett, 186). The lines are preceded in Allott's verse anthology by quotations from Drayton ('The greatest dangers promise greatest bliss') and Shakespeare, *Venus and Adonis*, 690 ('Danger deviseth shifts, wit waits on fear') (48). Oliver notes that the idea is proverbial, citing 'Danger and delight grow both upon one stalk' (Tilley, D28) and 'the more danger the more honour' (Tilley, D35).

39. *common*] ordinary, base, ignoble.

40. *hangs*] like fruit on a tree, within reach.

That like I best that flies beyond my reach.
Set me to scale the high pyramidès,
And thereon set the diadem of France;
I'll either rend it with my nails to naught
Or mount the top with my aspiring wings,   45
Although my downfall be the deepest hell.
For this I wake when others think I sleep.
For this I wait, that scorns attendance else.
For this my quenchless thirst whereon I build
Hath often pleaded kindred to the King.   50

---

42. *pyramidès*] pyramids of Egypt. In a letter to Ben Jonson, William Drummond notes that the emblem or *impressa* of the Cardinal of Lorraine, Guise's uncle, was 'a pyramid overgrown with ivy, the vulgar word, *te stante virebo* [I will grow while you are standing]' (Drummond, 396). The letter's editor remarks that 'The device described here traditionally implies the interrelationship of church (the ivy) and state (the pillar)' (396). Guise's image, then, which substitutes his own ambitious ascent for the growth of the ivy, might suggest the destructive and amoral force of his actions in a time of religious warfare that pitted church against state.

45–6.] The lines recall Icarus, who in Greek mythology fell to his death after hubristically flying too close to the sun with the waxen wings made by his father Daedalus (Grimal, 227). See Ovid, *Metamorphoses*, VIII.245–313. In his commentary on Icarus, Golding allegorises the myth as a warning against ambition: 'We also learn by Icarus how good it is to be / In mean estate and not to climb too high, but to agree / To wholesome counsel, for the hire of disobedience is / Repentance when it is too late forethinking things amiss' (Ovid, 'Epistle', 177–80). Marlowe alludes to this tragic myth throughout his plays, most notably in the Prologue to *Doctor Faustus*, which tells the audience that Faustus's 'waxen wings did mount above his reach, / And melting, heavens conspired his overthrow' (20–1).

47.] 'Watch thou, and wake when others be asleep, / To pry into the secrets of the state' (sig. A4ᵛ), York advises himself in *The First Part of the Contention* (1594).

48. *wait*] with the additional sense of waiting upon the King.

attendance] waiting, 'the action or condition of an inferior in waiting the leisure, convenience, or decision of a superior' (*OED*, n., 4).

else] otherwise.

49–50.] i.e. 'I have been led by my insatiable desire for the crown to claim kinship with the King.' Guise's cousin, Mary Queen of Scots, was married to Charles IX's older brother Francis II (r. 1559–60). As children, Guise,

SC. 2]   THE MASSACRE AT PARIS   59

    For this, this head, this heart, this hand and sword
    Contrives, imagines, and fully executes
    Matters of import aimed at by many
    Yet understood by none.
    For this hath heaven engendered me of earth;   55
    For this, this earth sustains my body's weight,
    And with this weight I'll counterpoise a crown
    Or with seditions weary all the world.
    For this from Spain the stately Catholics
    Send Indian gold to coin me French écus.   60
    For this have I a largesse from the Pope,
    A pension, and a dispensation too,
    And by that privilege to work upon
    My policy hath framed religion.

---

60. Send] *Dyce (subst);* Sends *O.*

Henry, Duke of Anjou, and Henry of Navarre were schoolmates for a year at Navarre College (Carroll, 185), and Guise had an affair with Margaret several years before her marriage to Navarre (Carroll, 188–9).
    51–2.] See 'As if he wanted hands, sense, sight, or heart, / He doth deviseth, sees nor dareth aught' (Kyd, *Cornelia*, 4.1.176–7).
    53. *import*] importance.
    57. *counterpoise*] counterbalance, be or supply the equivalent of. Although 'counterpoise a crown' may denote only Guise's desire to be the monarch's equal in power, the surrounding speech clearly indicates that Guise aims at the crown itself (see lines 40–3 and 85–7).
    stately] princely, noble, majestic (*OED*, adj., 1a).
    60. *Indian gold*] gold from the Americas.
    écus] French coins equivalent to English crowns (*OED*).
    61. *largesse*] generous gift of money.
    Pope] Pope Gregory XIII (1572–85).
    62. *pension*] regular stipend.
    dispensation] licence to commit ordinarily sinful deeds.
    64. *policy*] political strategy, cunning, scheming.
    framed] shaped, formed, adapted (*OED*, v., 5a, b).

Religion: *O Diabole!*
Fie, I am ashamed, however that I seem,
To think a word of such a simple sound
Of so great matter should be made the ground.
The gentle King, whose pleasure uncontrolled
Weak'neth his body and will waste his realm
If I repair not what he ruinates,
Him as a child I daily win with words,
So that for proof he barely bears the name.
I execute, and he sustains the blame.
The Mother Queen works wonders for my sake
And in my love entombs the hope of France,
Rifling the bowels of her treasury
To supply my wants and necessity.
Paris hath full five hundred colleges,
As monasteries, priories, abbeys, and halls,
Wherein are thirty thousand able men,
Besides a thousand sturdy student Catholics,
And more. Of my knowledge, in one cloister keep

---

83. And more. Of my] *Ribner (subst)*; And more of my *O.* keep] *Broughton (subst)*; keeps *O.*

65. O Diabole!] 'The Devil!' (Latin).
66–8.] i.e. 'I am ashamed when I consider that such a simple-sounding word as "religion" has been the cause of such great trouble.' Guise's trivialisation of religion in these lines, like his subordination of religion to policy in line 62, is Machiavellian. Compare Machevill's assertion at the beginning of *The Jew of Malta* that 'I count religion but a childish toy' (Prologue, 14). Earlier in the prologue, Machevill explicitly connects Guise to Machiavelli. 'Albeit the world think Machevill is dead, / Yet was his soul but flown beyond the Alps' (1–2), Machevill tells the audience, 'And, now the Guise is dead, is come from France' (3).
73.] i.e. so that the King exercises power in name only.
74.] See 'I lay the plot; he prosecutes the point', Kyd, *ST*, 3.4.40 (Oliver).
75. *Mother Queen*] Catherine.
76. *entombs*] encloses (*OED*, v., 2).
77. *bowels*] 'the interior of anything; heart, centre' (*OED*, n.1, 4).
79. *colleges*] religious houses.
80. *As*] such as.
83. *keep*] dwell.

Five hundred fat Franciscan friars and priests.
All this and more, if more may be comprised, 85
To bring the will of our desires to end.
Then, Guise, since thou hast all the cards
Within thy hands to shuffle or cut, take this as surest thing:
That, right or wrong, thou deal thyself a king.
Ay, but Navarre. Navarre, 'tis but a nook of France, 90
Sufficient yet for such a petty king
That with a rabblement of his heretics
Blinds Europe's eyes and troubleth our estate.
Him will we—

Pointing to his sword[.]

But first let's follow those in France 95
That hinder our possession to the crown.
As Caesar to his soldiers, so say I:
Those that hate me will I learn to loathe.
Give me a look that, when I bend the brows,
Pale death may walk in furrows of my face; 100
A hand that with a grasp may grip the world;
An ear to hear what my detractors say;

---

90. Ay] *Broughton (subst);* I *O.* 94.1. SD.] *printed on 92, aligned right, in O.* 101. grip] *O (gripe).*

85. *comprised*] laid hold of, taken, seized (*OED*, v., 1a).
86.] i.e. to accomplish the active intentions of my desires.
87–8.] Esche notes the occurrence of the playing card metaphor in Robert Greene's *Selimus* (1594). Unexpectedly given another opportunity to unseat his father Bajazet from the imperial throne of the Ottoman Empire, Selimus declaims, 'Will Fortune favour me yet once again, / And will she thrust the cards into my hands? / Well, if I chance but once to get the deck, / To deal and shuffle as I would, / Let Selim never see the daylight spring, / Unless I shuffle out myself a king' (17.1–6; Esche, 373).
90. *Navarre*] The small Kingdom of Navarre, with Pamplona as its capital city, was north of the Pyrenees, bordering both France and Spain.
95. *follow*] pursue.
97.] Guise was often compared to Caesar in contemporary Catholic pamphlet literature (Kocher, 'Contemporary Pamphlet Backgrounds', 155).

A royal seat, a sceptre, and a crown,
That those which do behold, they may become
As men that stand and gaze against the sun.   105
The plot is laid, and things shall come to pass
Where resolution strives for victory.   *Exit.*

[SCENE 3]

Enter the King of NAVARRE *and Queen* [MARGARET],
and his mother [*the* OLD] QUEEN, *the Prince of* CONDÉ,
the ADMIRAL, *and the* Apothecary *with the gloves, and*
[*he*] *gives them to the* OLD QUEEN.

Apothecary. Madam, I beseech Your Grace to accept this
    simple gift.
Old Queen. Thanks, my good friend. [*Gives him money*]
    Hold, take thou this reward.

Heading Sc. 3.] *Bullen (subst); not in* O.   1. SH. *Apothecary.*] *Ribner (subst);*
Pothe. O.   2. SH. *Old Queen.*] *Ribner (subst); Old Qu.* O.   2. SD. *Gives
him money*] *this edn; not in* O.

---

103. *seat*] throne.
105. *As ... sun*] i.e. blinded; see Dent S971.1, 'He that gazes upon the
sun shall at last be blind'. This is the only example cited. See *RII* 3.2.46–9:
Bolingbroke, Richard declares, '[s]hall see us rising in our throne' and, '[n]ot able to endure the sight of day', will 'tremble at his sin'.
    [Historically, and in Hotman, the death of the Queen of Navarre and the shooting of the Admiral were separate events, the former occurring several months before the wedding, on 9 June (Garrisson, *La Saint-Barthélemy*, 58). According to Hotman, the Queen 'died in the Court at Paris, of a sudden sickness' (*True and Plain Report*, xxxv) before the wedding, and only after an autopsy on her brain did the suspicion arise that she had been poisoned. The Admiral was shot on 'the 22 day of August, which was the fifth day after the King of Navarre's marriage' as he was returning from pleading the Huguenots' cause at King Charles's council: 'About noon, when he was in returning home from the council with a great company of noblemen and gentlemen, behold a harquebusier out of a window of a house near adjoining shot the Admiral with two bullets of lead through both the arms' (*True and Plain Report*, xl–xli). Hotman notes circumstantial evidence linking the assassination attempt to Guise (xlii) but does not connect him to the alleged poisoning of the Queen of Navarre.]
    2. *Hold*] wait, stay.

SC. 3] THE MASSACRE AT PARIS 63

Apothecary. I humbly thank Your Majesty. *Exit* Apothecary.
Old Queen. Methinks the gloves have a very strong perfume,
   The scent whereof doth make my head to ache.   5
Navarre. Doth not Your Grace know the man that gave
   them you?
Old Queen. Not well, but do remember such a man.
Admiral. Your Grace was ill-advised to take them, then,
   Considering of these dangerous times.
Old Queen. Help, son Navarre, I am poisoned!   10
Margaret. The heavens forbid Your Highness such mishap.
Navarre. The late suspicion of the Duke of Guise
   Might well have moved Your Highness to beware
   How you did meddle with such dangerous gifts.
Margaret. Too late it is, my lord, if that be true,   15
   To blame Her Highness, but I hope it be
   Only some natural passion makes her sick.
Old Queen. Oh no, sweet Margaret, the fatal poison
   Works within my head, my brainpan breaks,
   My heart doth faint, I die.   20

            She dies.

---

3. SH. *Apothecary.*] *Ribner (subst); Pothe. O.*   3. SD. Apothecary.] *Ribner (subst); Po. O.*   4. SH. *Old Queen.*] *Ribner (subst); Old Qu. O.*   6. SH. *Navarre.*] *Ribner (subst); Nauar. O.*   7. SH. *Old Queen.*] *Ribner (subst); Old Qu O.*   8. SH. *Admiral.*] *Ribner (subst); Ad. O.*   10. SH. *Old Queen.*] *Ribner (subst); Old Qu. O.*   11. SH. *Margaret.*] *Ribner (subst); Q Mar. O.*   12. SH. *Navarre.*] *Ribner (subst); Nauar. O.*   15. SH. *Margaret.*] *Ribner (subst); Q. Mar. O.*   18. SH. *Old Queen.*] *Ribner (subst); Old Qu O.*   20.1. SD.] printed on 20, aligned right, in *O.*

---

4. *perfume*] smell.
12.] i.e. our latest suspicions about Guise's plans to murder the Huguenots in Paris. See 1.31–4.
14. *meddle*] concern yourself, busy yourself, interfere (*OED*, v., 5, 6a).
17. *natural passion*] illness.
19. *brainpan*] skull. Hotman claims that the poison was not detected by the physicians who performed the initial autopsy on the Queen's body because it 'could not be espied by the physicians who did not open the head nor looked into the brain' (*True and Plain Report*, xxxv).

Navarre. My mother poisoned here before my face!
O gracious God, what times are these?
Oh grant, sweet God, my days may end with hers,
That I with her may die and live again.
Margaret. Let not this heavy chance, my dearest lord, 25
For whose effects my soul is massacred,
Infect thy gracious breast with fresh supply
To aggravate our sudden misery.
Admiral. Come, my lords, let us bear her body hence
And see it honoured with just solemnity. 30

As they are going, the Soldier *dischargeth his musket at the* LORD ADMIRAL.

Condé. What, are you hurt, my Lord High Admiral?
Admiral. Ay, my good lord, shot through the arm.
Navarre. We are betrayed. Come, my lords,
And let us go tell the King of this.
Admiral. These are the cursèd Guisians that do seek our death. 35
Oh, fatal was this marriage to us all.

They bear away the [OLD] QUEEN *and go out.*

---

21. SH. *Navarre.*] *Ribner (subst); Nauar. O.* 25. SH. *Margaret.*] *Ribner (subst); Q. Mar. O.* 26. For ... massacred,] *Dyce (subst);* (For ... massacred) *O.* 29. SH. *Admiral.*] *Ribner (subst); Ad. O.* 31. SH. *Condé.*] *Ribner (subst); Condy, O.* 31. Lord] *Broughton (subst);* L. *O.* 32. SH. *Admiral.*] *Ribner (subst); Admi. O.* 32. Ay] *Broughton (subst);* I *O.* 33. SH. *Navarre.*] *Ribner (subst); Nauar. O.* 33–4. lords, / And] *Broughton (subst);* Lords, and *O.* 35. SH. *Admiral.*] *Ribner (subst); Admi. O.* 36.1. SD.] *centred O.*

---

24. *live again*] i.e. live again in heaven.
25. *heavy chance*] sorrowful occurrence.
26. *For whose effects*] because of which.
27. *supply*] reinforcements, troops (*OED*, n., 5).
30. *just solemnity*] proper funeral rites.
36.] 'Fatal is this marriage, cancelling our states' (sig. A3ʳ), Humphrey Duke of Gloucester declares of the marriage between Henry VI and Lady Margaret in *The First Part of the Contention.*

[SCENE 4]

Enter the King [CHARLES], QUEEN MOTHER
[CATHERINE], *Duke of* GUISE, Duke ANJOU,
[*and*] Duke DUMAINE.

Catherine. My noble son, and princely Duke of Guise,
Now have we got the fatal straggling deer
Within the compass of a deadly toil,
And as we late decreed we may perform.
Charles. Madam, it will be noted through the world   5

Heading Sc. 4.] *Bullen (subst); not in O.*   0.1. SD. ANJOU] *O (*Anioy*).*
Modernised silently throughout.   0.2. SD. DUMAINE] *O (*Demayne*).*
Modernised silently throughout.   1. SH. *Catherine.*] *Ribner (subst);* Queene
Mother. *O.*   5. SH. *Charles.*] *Ribner (subst);* King. *O.*

[Scene 4 begins with the royal council in Catherine's gardens at Tuileries, her palace in Paris, from which the scene transitions, through the dramatically economical device of thrusting the Admiral on stage in his bed, to Charles's visit to the wounded Huguenot leader. Marlowe takes many of his details from his source but has rearranged the events chronologically. In Hotman, the King is playing tennis with Guise and Navarre when he receives the news of the assassination attempt (*True and Plain Report*, xli), and the royal council takes place the day after Charles visits the Admiral. Modern historians accept Hotman's account, placing the visit in the afternoon of 22 August and the council in the evening of 23 August (Jouanna, 76, 97). Hotman does not list Guise as a participant in the meetings at Tuileries, although modern historians state that he was present at at least some of them (Garrisson, *La Saint-Barthélemy*, 93; Carroll, 213). According to Hotman, the council consisted of Catherine, Charles, the Duke of Anjou, Tavannes, Retz, and Gonzague (*True and Plain Report*, xlix).]

1. *son*] Charles IX.
2–4.] In Hotman, Catherine 'showed them how those whom they had long been in wait for were now sure in hold ... so as they were so snared that they could no way escape, and the captains taken thus, it was not to be feared that any of the Religion would from thenceforth stir anymore' (*True and Plain Report*, xlix).
2. *fatal*] doomed (*OED*, adj., 2, citing this line).
straggling] wandering, straying (*OED*, v.1, 1a).
3. *toil*] See note to 1.53.
4. *decreed*] decided (i.e. to massacre the Huguenots in Paris). See 1.31–4.
5–6.] Charles here anticipates the opinion of the Court after the massacre: according to Hotman, 'many of the Court secretly muttered that the King should by this fact incur dishonour, not only among foreign nations but also with all posterity in time to come forever' (*True and Plain Report*, lxxvii).
5. *noted*] branded, condemned, stigmatised (*OED*, v.2, 3b, c).

> An action bloody and tyrannical,
> Chiefly since under safety of our word
> They justly challenge their protection.
> Besides, my heart relents that noblemen
> Only corrupted in religion, 10
> Ladies of honour, knights, and gentlemen
> Should for their conscience taste such ruthless ends.
> *Anjou.* Though gentle minds should pity others' pains,
> Yet will the wisest note their proper griefs
> And rather seek to scourge their enemies 15
> Than be themselves base subjects to the whip.
> *Guise.* Methinks, my lord, Anjou hath well advised
> Your Highness to consider of the thing
> And rather choose to seek your country's good
> Than pity or relieve these upstart heretics. 20
> *Catherine.* I hope these reasons may serve my princely son
> To have some care for fear of enemies.
> *Charles.* Well, madam, I refer it to Your Majesty
> And to my nephew here, the Duke of Guise.
> What you determine I will ratify. 25

10–12. Only ... religion, / Ladies ... gentlemen, / Should ... ends.] *Broughton (subst);* Onely ... honor, / Knightes ... ends. *O.* 16. Than] *Robinson (subst);* Then *O.* 20. Than] *Broughton (subst);* Then *O.* 23. SH. Charles.] *Ribner (subst); King. O.*

---

7. *our word*] According to Hotman, in the months leading up to the marriage the King gave the wary Huguenots several verbal reassurances that they would be safe in Paris during the wedding festivities (*True and Plain Report*, xxx).

8. *They*] the Huguenots.

challenge] lay claim to, demand as a right (*OED*, v., 5).

9. *relents*] dissolves, melts, softens (*OED*, v.1, 2).

13. SH. Anjou] Henry, Duke of Anjou (1551–89). Anjou was Charles IX's younger brother and next in line to the throne. He reigned as Henry III from 1574 to 1589.

13. *gentle*] also, noble.

14. *proper*] own.

16. *base*] mean, ignoble.

24. *nephew*] 'kinsman' (Oliver, 107). Guise was not Charles's nephew. See note to 2.47–8.

25. *What ... ratify*] i.e. 'I will approve what you decide'.

SC. 4] THE MASSACRE AT PARIS 67

Catherine. Thanks to my princely son. Then tell me, Guise,
  What order will you set down for the massacre?
Guise. Thus, madam.
  They that shall be actors in this massacre
  Shall wear white crosses on their burgonets 30
  And tie white linen scarfs about their arms.
  He that wants these and is suspected of heresy
  Shall die, be he king or emperor.
  Then I'll have a peal of ordnance shot from the tower,
  At which they all shall issue out and set the streets, 35
  And then, the watchword being given, a bell shall ring,
  Which, when they hear, they shall begin to kill
  And never cease until that bell shall cease,
  Then breathe awhile.

Enter the Admiral's Man.

Charles.   How now, fellow, what news?
Man. An it please Your Grace, the Lord High Admiral, 40
  Riding the streets, was traitorously shot
  And most humbly entreats Your Majesty
  To visit him sick in his bed.

---

39. SH. *Charles.*] *Ribner (subst); King. O.*   40. An] *Broughton (subst);* And *O.*   42. humbly] *Broughton (subst);* humble *O.*

27.] Hotman claims that the council decided that 'the ordering and doing of all should be committed to the Duke of Guise' (*True and Plain Report*, l).
  30. *white ... burgonets*] In Hotman, 'a white cross pinned upon their caps' (*True and Plain Report*, lii).
  burgonets] light steel helmets worn by infantry, particularly pikemen (*OED*, n.).
  31. *white ... arms*] In Hotman, 'a white linen cloth hanged about their left arm' (*True and Plain Report*, lii).
  32. *wants*] lacks.
  34. *peal of ordnance*] cannon fire.
  35. *set ... streets*] post or station themselves in the streets (*OED*, v.1).
  36. *a ... ring*] According to Hotman, 'the token to set upon them, should be given ... with a tocsin or ringing of the great bell of the palace' (*True and Plain Report*, lii).
  watchword] signal.
  40. *An*] if.

68   THE MASSACRE AT PARIS   [SC. 4

Charles. Messenger, tell him I will see him straight.
                                                     Exit Admiral's Man.
What shall we do now with the Admiral?   45
Catherine. Your Majesty were best go visit him
   And make a show as if all were well.
Charles. Content. I will go visit the Admiral.
Guise. And I will go take order for his death.   *Exit* GUISE.

              Enter the ADMIRAL *in his bed.*

Charles. How fares it with my Lord High Admiral?   50
   Hath he been hurt with villains in the street?
   I vow and swear, as I am King of France,
   To find and to repay the man with death,
   With death delayed and torments never used,
   That durst presume for hope of any gain   55
   To hurt the nobleman their sovereign loves.

---

44. SH. *Charles.*] *Ribner (subst); King. O.*   44.1. SD. *Admiral's* Man] *Oliver (subst); Messenger O.*   46. SH. *Catherine.*] *Ribner (subst); Qu. O.*   48. SH. *Charles.*] *Ribner (subst); King. O.*   50. SH. *Charles.*] *Ribner (subst); King. O.*

   44. *straight*] immediately.
   48. *I ... Admiral*] Hotman states that Catherine, Anjou, and others who 'afterward were chief ringleaders in the butchery of Paris' (*True and Plain Report*, xliiii) accompanied Charles.
   49.1. SD.] A scene break at this point is unnecessary. Oliver comments that 'Editors who emended O's "Exit Guise" to "Exeunt" and started a new "scene" here failed to appreciate the continuity and fluidity of the action on the Elizabethan public stage' (108). During production at the Rose, the play's original performance venue, the Admiral was probably pushed on to the stage in a bed through a central entrance, probably curtained, in the tiring house façade. In her survey of stage directions involving beds in plays between 1580 and 1642, Leslie Thomson concludes that '*enter in bed* and *drawn out in bed* both mean that the property was to be brought out of the tiring house and placed forward on the stage' ('Beds', 33). In line with his earlier statement that 'I will go visit the Admiral' (47), Charles would then have approached the bed, either by himself or (in keeping with Hotman) accompanied by Catherine and the other characters remaining on stage. If Catherine and the others do not accompany Charles, they might exit with Guise.
   51. *with*] by.
   52–6.] 'The hurt, my Admiral, is done to thee,' Hotman's Charles declares, 'but the dishonour to me. But by the death of God (saith he) I swear I will so severely revenge both the hurt and the dishonour that it shall never be forgotten' (*True and Plain Report*, xliiii).
   55. *durst*] dares.

Admiral. Ah, my good lord, these are the Guisians
 That seek to massacre our guiltless lives.
Charles. Assure yourself, my good Lord Admiral,
 I deeply sorrow for your treacherous wrong   60
 And that I am not more secure myself
 Than I am careful you should be preserved.
 Cosseins!

[*Enter* COSSEINS.]

 Take twenty of our strongest guard
 And under your direction see they keep
 All treacherous violence from our noble friend,   65
 Repaying all attempts with present death
 Upon the cursèd breakers of our peace.
 And so, be patient, good Lord Admiral,
 And every hour I will visit you.
Admiral. I humbly thank Your royal Majesty.   70
 Exeunt omnes.

---

57. SH. *Admiral.*] Ribner (subst); *Ad. O.*   59. SH. *Charles.*] Ribner (subst); *King. O.*   62. Than] Broughton (subst); Then *O.*   63. Cosseins] *O* (Cosin). Modernised silently throughout.   Cosseins!] Ribner (subst); Cosin, *O.*   63.1. SD. *Enter* COSSEINS.] this edn; not in *O.*   70. SH. *Admiral.*] Ribner (subst); *Admi. O.*

57-8.] In Hotman the Admiral makes the same accusation: 'it was no doubt (said he) that this good turn was done him by the Duke of Guise' (*True and Plain Report*, xlv).

58. *massacre*] make a general slaughter or carnage of (*OED*, v., 1a, citing this line).

61-2.] i.e., in Hotman's words, that the King 'was fully determined to provide as well for the Admiral's safety as for his own' (*True and Plain Report*, xlvii).

63. *Cosseins*] captain of the royal guard (Garrisson, *La Saint-Barthélemy*, 89). Dyce, Bullen, and other early editors read O's 'Cosin' as 'Cousin'. Bennett, however, observes that 'Cosin' is clearly the name of the captain, citing Hotman's *Life of Coligny* (Bennett, 196). In *True and Plain Report*, Hotman observes that 'There could hardly a man be found more hateful against the Admiral's part nor more affected to the Guisians than this Cossin' (xlviii).

66. *present*] instant.

[SCENE 5]

Enter GUISE, ANJOU, DUMAINE, GONZAGUE, RETZ,
MONTSOREAU, *and* Soldiers *to the massacre.*

Guise. Anjou, Dumaine, Gonzague, Retz,
  Swear by the argent crosses in your burgonets
  To kill all that you suspect of heresy.
Dumaine. I swear by this to be unmerciful.
Anjou. I am disguised, and none knows who I am,   5
  And therefore mean to murder all I meet.
Gonzague. And so will I.
Retz.   And I.
Guise. Away then, break into the Admiral's house.
Retz. Ay, let the Admiral be first dispatched.
Guise. The Admiral,   10
  Chief standard-bearer to the Lutherans,
  Shall in the entrance of this massacre
  Be murdered in his bed. Gonzague,
  Conduct them thither and then beset his house,
  That not a man may live.   15

Heading Sc. 5.] *Greg (subst); not in* O.   0.1. SD. GONZAGUE] *O (*Gonzago*)*.
Modernised silently throughout.   RETZ] *O (*Retes*). Modernised silently throughout.*   MONTSOREAU] *O (*Montsorrell*). Modernised silently throughout.*   7.
SH. *Gonzague.*] *Ribner (subst); Gonza.* O.   9. Ay] *Broughton (subst);* I *O.*
10–11. Admiral, / Chief] *Broughton (subst);* Admirall cheefe *O.*   13–14. Be
… Gonzague, / Conduct] *Brooke (subst); Gonzago* conduct *O.*   14–15. house,
/ That] *this edn;* house that *O.*

[The massacre began before dawn on 24 August with the murder of the Admiral in his lodgings on the rue de Béthisy and the slaughter of Huguenot nobles lodged in the Louvre (Jouanna, 110). In *True and Plain Report* Hotman provides an extended narrative of the murder (lii–lvii), whose broad outlines Marlowe follows in this scene. Hotman, however, does not name either Anjou or Dumaine as being present alongside Guise when the murder was committed. Guise's companion was, rather, 'the bastard son of King Henry [Henry II] , commonly called the Chevalier' (*True and Plain Report*, lii).]
  1. *Gonzague*] Louis de Gonzague (1539–95), Prince of Mantoue and Duke of Nevers (Garrisson, *La Saint-Barthélemy*, 93).
  Retz] Albert Gondi (1522–1602), Count of Retz (Garrisson, *La Saint-Barthélemy*, 91).
  2. *argent*] silver.
  11. *standard-bearer*] flag-carrier, leader.
  12. *entrance*] beginning.

SC. 5]   THE MASSACRE AT PARIS   71

Anjou. That charge is mine. Switzers, keep you the streets,
    And at each corner shall the King's guard stand.
Gonzague. Come, sirs, follow me.
              Exit GONZAGUE *and others with him.*
Anjou. Cosseins, the captain of the Admiral's guard
    Placed by my brother, will betray his lord.   20
    Now, Guise, shall Catholics flourish once again:
    The head being off, the members cannot stand.
Retz. But look, my lord, there's some in the Admiral's house.

       Enter [GONZAGUE *and others*] *into the* ADMIRAL'S
                    house, and he in his bed.

Anjou. In lucky time. Come, let us keep this lane
    And slay his servants that shall issue out.   25
Gonzague. Where is the Admiral?

23.1. SD.] *aligned right O.* GONZAGUE *and others*] *Bullen (subst); not in O.*
26. SH. *Gonzague.*] *Ribner (subst); Gonza, O.*

---

  16. *That charge*] i.e. cordoning off the Admiral's house.
Switzers] Swiss mercenaries.
keep] defend, watch over.
  19. *Admiral's*] Cosseins was captain of the royal guard, but in the previous scene Charles puts him in charge of protecting the Admiral (4.63–5).
  22. *The ... stand*] Proverbial (Dent, 257.1).
  23.1. SD.] The Admiral's house could be represented by the same 'discovery space' from which the Admiral might have 'enter[ed] ... in his bed' (49.2 SD) in the previous scene. Alternatively, after having exited the stage's main level at line 18, Gonzague and his soldiers might re-enter on the upper stage, as Oliver suggests (111). As Evelyn Tribble notes, 'the dialogue' that culminates in Guise's command to 'throw him [the Admiral's body] down' at line 32 'seems to imply transactions between two levels of action: the main platform stage and space above' (63). Leslie Thomson, however, states that 'the evidence provided by stage directions in other plays of the period indicates that (not surprisingly) beds were never located above; furthermore, the phrasing of the first direction puts the bed in or before the discovery space, and it is virtually impossible to imagine that it could have been moved to the upper level in the few minutes it took to perform the first twenty-three lines of the next scene before the bed reappears' ('Staging', 32). Citing Thomson, Tribble concludes that 'It seems likely, then, that the main acting area was imaginatively and kinetically transformed into two levels' (63).
  24. *lane*] one might imagine the 'lane' to be on the peripheries of the staging area having been chosen to represent the Admiral's house, on the side or front of the stage and close enough to the door of the Admiral's house to allow Anjou and his men to 'slay his servants that shall issue out' (25).

72   THE MASSACRE AT PARIS   [SC. 5

Admiral. Oh, let me pray before I die.
Gonzague. Then pray unto our Lady. Kiss this cross!

[*He*] *stab*[s] *him*[.]

Admiral. O God, forgive my sins.
Guise. Gonzague, what, is he dead?   30
Gonzague. Ay, my lord.
Guise. Then throw him down.

[*The body of the* ADMIRAL *is thrown down.*]

Anjou. Now, cousin, view him well.
    It may be it is some other, and he escaped.
Guise. Cousin, 'tis he. I know him by his look.   35
    See where my soldier shot him through the arm.
    He missed him near, but we have struck him now.

---

27. SH. *Admiral.*] *Ribner (subst); Admi. O.*   28. SH. *Gonzague.*] *Ribner (subst); Gonza. O.*   28.1. SD.] *printed on 28, aligned right, in O.*   29. SH. *Admiral.*] *Ribner (subst); Admi. O.*   30. SH. *Guise.*] *Broughton (subst); Guise, O.*   31. SH. *Gonzague.*] *Ribner (subst); Gonza. O.*   31. Ay] *Broughton (subst);* I *O.*   32.1. SD.] *Oliver (subst); not in O.*   33–4. well. / It] *this edn;* well, it *O;* well; / It *Broughton (subst).*

27.] In Hotman, the Admiral's dying words are a plea for his life: 'young man, consider my age and the weak case that I am now in' (*True and Plain Report*, lv). The line echoes *The True Tragedy of Richard Duke of York* (1595), 'Oh, let me pray before I take my death' (sig. A8ʳ).

28. *our Lady*] the Virgin Mary. Protestants considered it idolatry to pray to Mary and other saints rather than directly to God.

this cross] Gonzague's sword. Oliver notes the grim humour of this, which he states is 'characteristic of Marlowe' (111).

32.1. SD.] If the assassination of the Admiral has taken place on the upper stage, a dummy could have been used for the Admiral's body. The use of a dummy would also have facilitated the stage action indicated at line 41 (Guise stamps on the body) and 42 (the body with the head and hands cut off). Nonetheless, as Thomson remarks, 'it is entirely possible to interpret "throw him down" to mean simply that Gonzago throws the body from the bed to the stage in a final act of disrespect' ('Staging', 32). Dessen and Thomson catalogue the variety of actions that the stage direction 'throw' could imply: '(1) *throwing* of properties (2) the *throwing* off of a disguise (3) the *throwing* down of one figure by another (4) other distinctive stage business' (229).

35. *I ... look*] According to Hotman, after wiping the blood off the body's face, Guise 'said, "Now I know him, it is he"' (*True and Plain Report*, lvi).

37. *near*] not by much, just.

SC. 5] THE MASSACRE AT PARIS 73

    Ah, base Châtillon and degenerate,
    Chief standard-bearer to the Lutherans,
    Thus, in despite of thy religion,   40
    The Duke of Guise stamps on thy lifeless bulk.
Anjou. Away with him. Cut off his head and hands
    And send them for a present to the Pope.
    And when this just revenge is finished,
    Unto Mount Faucon will we drag his corpse,   45
    And he that, living, hated so the cross
    Shall, being dead, be hanged thereon in chains.
    [*1 Soldier* and *2 Soldier cut off the body's head and hands
                                          then exit with the body.*]
Guise. Anjou, Gonzague, Retz, if that you three
    Will be as resolute as I and Dumaine,
    There shall not a Huguenot breathe in France.   50
Anjou. I swear by this cross, we'll not be partial
    But slay as many as we can come near.

---

38. Châtillon] *O* (*Shatillian*). 38–9. degenerate, / Chief] Broughton (*subst*); degenerate, cheef *O*. 47.1. SD.] this edn; not in *O*.

---

   38. *Châtillon*] the Lord High Admiral.
   41.] Hotman does not mention Guise stamping on the Admiral's body in *True and Plain Report*, but in his biography of the Admiral he relates that 'The Admiral's body, being thrown down out of a window, was trampled underfoot by the young Duke of Guise' (*Life*, H2^v). Other sources available to Marlowe, such as *Mémoires de l'état de France sous Charles neuvième* (1576), also contain this detail (Thomas and Tydeman, 253).
   42–3. *Cut ... Pope*] Hotman recounts that 'a certain Italian of Gonzague's band cut off the Admiral's head and sent it preserved with spices to Rome to the Pope and the Cardinal of Lorraine. Other cut off his hands, and other his secret parts' (*True and Plain Report*, lvi).
   45. *Mount Faucon*] A hill near Paris that served as the French crown's main site for criminal executions and where bodies were left to decay on the gibbets. Although he does not name the gallows in *True and Plain Report*, in *Life of Coligny* Hotman narrates that after Guise had stamped on it, the Admiral's body was 'tumbled into the mire in the open street and mangled and used with all the villainy that might be, and three days after carried out of the city by the furious multitude and hanged up by the feet upon the gallows of Mountfalcon' (H2^v).
   47. *thereon*] i.e. from one of Mount Faucon's gibbets, from which the bodies of executed criminals were suspended.
   51. *partial*] biased, prejudiced, unfair (*OED*, adj., 4a).

Guise. Montsoreau, go shoot the ordnance off,
  That they which have already set the street
  May know their watchword, then toll the bell, 55
  And so let's forward to the massacre.
Montsoreau. I will, my lord.   *Exit* MONTSOREAU.
Guise. And now, my lords, let us closely to our business.
Anjou. Anjou will follow thee.
Dumaine.   And so will Dumaine.

   The ordnance being shot off, the bell tolls.

Guise. Come then, let's away. 60
                            Exeunt.

[SCENE 6]

The GUISE *enters again, with all the rest, with their
swords drawn, chasing the Protestants.*

Guise. Tuez, tuez, tuez!
  Let none escape, murder the Huguenots.
Anjou. Kill them, kill them!
                            Exeunt.

---

57. SH. *Montsoreau.*] *Ribner (subst); Mount.* O.   57. SD. MONTSOREAU.] *Ribner (subst);* Mount. O.   59. SH. *Dumaine.*] *Ribner (subst); Du.* O.   59.1. SD.] *aligned right* O.

Heading Sc. 6] *Oliver (subst); not in* O.   1–2. *tuez!* / Let] *Dyce (subst); tue, let* O.   3.1. SD.] *printed on 3, aligned right, in* O.

---

53. *Montsoreau*] Jean de Chambes (1530–75), Count of Montsoreau, whom Hotman describes as 'a most cruel enemy of the Religion' (*True and Plain Report*, lxxvi), perhaps because in 1568 the Huguenots sacked his castle in Montsoreau.
ordnance] cannon.
54. *set ... street*] i.e. taken their positions in the street.
55. *bell*] the bells of the church of Saint-Germain-l'Auxerrois and the Palace of Justice (Jouanna, 112).
58. *closely*] secretly, covertly (*OED*, adv., 3).

[Once done murdering the Admiral, the men under Guise's command cross the Seine and attack the Huguenots lodged in the Left Bank neighbourhood of Saint-Germain-de-Prés (Jouanna, 112).]
  1. Tuez, tuez, tuez!] 'Kill, kill, kill!' (French).

[SCENE 7]

Enter LÉRAN *running, the* GUISE *and the rest pursuing him.*

Guise. Léran, Léran, follow Léran! Sirrah,
Are you a preacher of these heresies?
Léran. I am a preacher of the Word of God,
And thou a traitor to thy soul and Him.
Guise. Dearly beloved brother, thus 'tis written.   5

He stabs him.

Anjou. Stay, my lord, let me begin the psalm.
Guise. Come, drag him away and throw him in a ditch.
Exeunt.

Heading Sc. 7] *Oliver (subst); not in O.*
0.1. SD. LÉRAN] *O (Loreine). Modernised silently throughout.*

[In Hotman, Léran is assaulted in the Louvre, and not by Guise. Rather, he and a Monsieur de Pilles are dragged from Navarre's quarters, where Navarre has hidden them, and attacked. De Pilles is slaughtered, but Léran, 'being thrust through with a sword, escaped and ran into the Queen of Navarre's [Margaret's] chamber, and was by her kept and preserved from the violence of those that pursued him. Shortly after, she obtained his pardon of her brother, and committing him to her own physicians restored him to both life and health' (*True and Plain Report*, lxi). Margaret de Valois records the incident in her memoirs (*Memoirs*, 47). Guise's presence and his command that his men 'throw him [Léran's body] in a ditch' (7) suggests that Marlowe has relocated this murder to the streets of Saint-Germain-de-Prés.]

1. *Léran*] Gabriel de Lévis, seigneur de Léran (Jouanna, 111).

Sirrah] condescending form of address, roughly equivalent to 'boy'. Usually used to assert social superiority.

5.] Guise here parodies a common opening formula of Protestant scripture readings and sermons. Esche observes that a similar parody of Puritan forms of speech is found in *Doctor Faustus*. In response to the two scholars' inquiry regarding Faustus's whereabouts, Wagner 'will set my countenance like a Precisian and begin to speak thus: "Truly, my dear brethren, my master is within at dinner ... and so the Lord bless you, preserve you, and keep you, my dear brethren"' (1.2.21–6; Esche, 380).

6. *begin the psalm*] Anjou continues Guise's parody of Protestant liturgy, in which the congregational singing of psalms played an important role.

76   THE MASSACRE AT PARIS   [SC. 8

[SCENE 8]

Enter MONTSOREAU *and knocks at* SEROUNE'S *door.*

Seroune's Wife. Who is that which knocks there?
Montsoreau. Montsoreau, from the Duke of Guise.
Seroune's Wife. Husband, come down. Here's one would speak
   with you from the Duke of Guise.

Enter SEROUNE.

Seroune. To speak with me from such a man as he?   5
Montsoreau. Ay, ay, for this, Seroune, and thou shalt ha't.

S*howing his dagger.*

Seroune. Oh, let me pray before I take my death.
Montsoreau. Dispatch, then, quickly.
Seroune. O Christ my Saviour.
Montsoreau. Christ, villain! Why dar'st thou presume to call   10
   on Christ without the intercession of some saint? *Sanctus
   Iacobus*, he was my saint, pray to him.

Heading Sc. 8] *Bullen (subst); not in O.*   2. SH. *Montsoreau.*] *Ribner (subst);
Mount. O.*   3. SH. *Seroune's Wife.*] *Broughton (subst); Wife. O.*   6. SH.
Montsoreau.] *Ribner (subst); Mount. O.*   6. Ay, ay] *Broughton (subst);* I,
I *O.*   6.1. SD.] *printed on 6, aligned right, in O. Showing*] *O (shewing).*
8. SH. *Montsoreau.*] *Ribner (subst); Mount. O.*   10. SH. *Montsoreau.*] *Ribner
(subst); Mount. O.*   11. *Sanctus*] *Broughton (subst); Sancta O.*

   [If Kocher's argument that this scene is modelled on an incident in
Hotman in which Montsoreau rides to Angiers and murders a man called
Masson de Rivers is correct (Kocher, 'François Hotman', 363), then it might
be contended that the scene would be better placed after the following scene,
at the end of which Guise commands the spread of the massacre into other
French municipalities: 'Gonzague, post you to Orléans, / Retz to Dieppe,
Montsoreau unto Rouen' (83–4). Nothing in the scene, however, indicates
a shift in locale from somewhere in Paris. Hotman describes Masson as 'a
pastor of the Church and esteemed a singular man both in virtuousness of
life and in excellency of wit and learning' (*True and Plain Report*, lxxvi).]
   6. *ha't*] have it.
   7.] This line and line 12 echo *The True Tragedy*, 'Oh, let me pray before
I take my death' (sig. A8ᵛ).
   11. Sanctus Iacobus] Saint James, patron saint of soldiers (Farmer, 464).
Oliver comments that '[t]he doctrinal point of Mountsorrell's gibe is, of
course, to "justify" the murder of the man who, against normal Catholic
practice, insists on pleading directly with the Father or the Son' (115).

[SC. 9] THE MASSACRE AT PARIS 77

Seroune. Oh, let me pray unto my God.
Montsoreau. Then take this with you.

[*He*] *stab*[*s*] *him.*

Exit.

[SCENE 9]

Enter RAMUS *in his study.*

Ramus. What fearful cries come from the river Seine,
That fright poor Ramus sitting at his book?

---

13. SH. *Montsoreau.*] *Ribner (subst); Mount. O.* 13.1. SD.] *printed on 13, aligned right, in O.*

Heading Sc. 9] *Bullen (subst); not in O.* 1. come] *Broughton (subst);* comes *O.* Seine] *conj Malone, Broughton (subst);* Rene *O.* 2. fright] *Broughton (subst);* frightes *O.*

[Paris remains the scene: Ramus's lodgings on the Left Bank, then the Louvre. Hotman mentions Ramus only in passing as a massacre victim (*True and Plain Report*, lxxiiii). Other sources available to Marlowe, such as Goulart's *Mémoires de l'etat de France* (1576–77), provide more detailed accounts of Ramus's murder. Goulart relates that Ramus attempted to hide in the college of Presles and 'when he was discovered, he paid a large sum to save his life. Notwithstanding, he was murdered, and thrown down out of an upstairs window so that his entrails spilled out over the stones; then the entrails were dragged through the streets, and the body whipped by some students urged on by their masters, to the great disgrace of the very learning which Ramus had made his profession' (qtd Thomas and Tydeman, 277). Hotman describes the murder of Navarre and Condé's tutors as follows: they 'were thrust out of the chamber and by the King's guard of Switzers hewed in pieces and slaughtered in the King's own sight' (*True and Plain Report*, lix). Historically, two separate groups of soldiers initiated the massacres on the morning of 24 August, the first under Guise, charged with eliminating the Admiral and the Huguenots lodged in the neighbourhood of Saint-Germain-de-Prés, and the second composed of the King's Swiss and French guards, charged with executing the Huguenots lodged in the Louvre (Jouanna, 109–12).]

0. SD. in his study] The 'discovery space' or 'inner stage', situated at the back of open-air amphitheatres such as the Rose and the Globe, could have served as Ramus's study. See Introduction, pp. 40–1.

1. SH. Ramus] Pierre de la Ramée (1515–72). Professor at Collège Royal from 1551, Ramus was a French philosopher whose attempts to reform Aristotelian logic, the foundation of early modern European university education, drew the ire of his more conservative academic contemporaries.

78   THE MASSACRE AT PARIS   [SC. 9

    I fear the Guisians have passed the bridge
And mean once more to menace me.

Enter TALEUS.

Taleus. Fly, Ramus, fly, if thou wilt save thy life!   5
Ramus. Tell me, Taleus, wherefore should I fly?
Taleus. The Guisians are hard at thy door
    And mean to murder us. Hark, hark, they come!
    I'll leap out at the window.
Ramus. Sweet Taleus, stay.   10

Enter GONZAGUE *and* RETZ.

Gonzague. Who goes there?
Retz. 'Tis Taleus, Ramus' bedfellow.
Gonzague. What art thou?
Taleus. I am, as Ramus is, a Christian.
Retz. Oh, let him go. He is a Catholic.   15

Exit TALEUS.

7–8. door / And] *Bowers (subst);* doore, and *O.* 8–9. come! / I'll] *this edn;* come, Ile *O.* 13. SH. Gonzague.] *Ribner (subst);* Gonza. *O.* 14. SH. Taleus.] *Broughton (subst); Tal. O.* 15. SH. Retz.] *Broughton (subst); Ret. O.* 15.1. SD.] *Broughton (subst); Enter* Ramus. *[centred] Exit* Taleus. *in O.*

Marlowe would have been familiar with Ramist logic from his time at Cambridge University, where Ramist logic had numerous proponents. Ramus converted to Calvinism in 1561 (Schmitt and Skinner, 834). English Protestants considered him to be a martyr (he is mentioned in Foxe's *Acts and Monuments* in a list of 'learned men' murdered in the massacres). In the 1580s and 1590s, however, Thomas Nashe and others turned Ramus into a satirical figure associated with Puritanism and reductive learning (Knight, 53–65).

    1. *Seine*] Paris's major river.

    3. *bridge*] The Admiral's murder took place in the rue de Béthisy, on Paris's Right Bank. After the Admiral's murder, Guise and his men crossed over the Ile de la Cité into the Latin Quarter of Paris's Left Bank, where Ramus resided. Three bridges connected the Ile de la Cité and the Left Bank: the Petit Pont, the Pont Saint-Michel, and the Pont aux Meuniers (Carroll, 215–17).

    4. *once more*] The phrase might suggest that Ramus escaped the earlier stages of the massacre by fleeing across the bridge to his house or that he and the Guises have a history of conflict.

    5. SH. Taleus] Omer Talon (1510–62), Ramus's friend and collaborator.

    6. *wherefore*] why.

    12. *bedfellow*] In this period room-mates often shared a bed.

Gonzague. Come, Ramus, more gold, or thou shalt have the
    stab.
Ramus. Alas, I am a scholar. How should I have gold?
    All that I have is but my stipend from the King,
    Which is no sooner received but it is spent.

        Enter the GUISE[, DUMAINE,] *and* ANJOU.

Anjou. Who have you there? 20
Retz. 'Tis Ramus, the King's Professor of Logic.
Guise. Stab him.
Ramus. O good my lord, wherein hath Ramus been so
    offencious?
Guise. Marry, sir, in having a smack in all
    And yet didst never sound anything to the depth. 25
    Was it not thou that scoff'dst the *Organon*
    And said it was a heap of vanities?
    He that will be flat dichotomist
    And seen in nothing but epitomes
    Is in your judgement thought a learnèd man, 30
    And he forsooth must go and preach in Germany,

---

16. SH. *Gonzague.*] Ribner (subst); *Gon. O.* 21. SH. *Retz.*] Broughton (subst); *Ret. O.* 22. SH. *Guise.*] Broughton (subst); *Guise, O.* 26. scoff'dst] Broughton (subst); scoftes *O.*

---

16. *more gold*] Gonzague's demand for 'more gold' could imply that Ramus escaped the menaces to which he refers in line 4 by bribery.
23. *offencious*] offending. *OED* cites this usage as the sole instance.
24. *smack*] smattering, superficial knowledge.
all] i.e. all knowledge.
25. *sound*] measure, take the measure of.
26. Organon] Collectively, Aristotle's six treatises on logic. These lines echo the A-text opening of *Faustus*.
28. *flat dichotomist*] i.e. one who, like Ramus, reduces logic to the dichotomies produced by a statement and its negation. Oliver glosses 'flat' as 'unswerving, uncompromising'.
29. *seen*] learned, knowledgeable.
epitomes] summaries.
31–2.] i.e. equipped with Ramus's new, anti-Aristotelian logic, the 'flat dichotomist' is ready to become a Protestant activist in the heartland of the Reformation, Germany, and take on the learned Catholic doctors, for whose thought Aristotle provided the orthodox philosophical foundation. Ramus taught for a while at the University of Heidelberg.
31. *forsooth*] truly, verily, indeed.

Excepting against doctors' actions
And *ipse dixi* with this quiddity:
Argumentum testimonii est inartificiale.
To contradict which, I say 'Ramus shall die'. 35
How answer you that? Your *nego argumentum*
Cannot serve, sirrah. Kill him.
Ramus. O good my lord, let me but speak a word.
Anjou. Well, say on.
Ramus. Not for my life do I desire this pause, 40
But in my latter hour to purge myself,
In that I know the things that I have writ,
Which, as I hear, one Shekins takes it ill
Because my places, being but three, contain all his.
I knew the *Organon* to be confused, 45

---

33. *ipse*] *conj Malone, Robinson (subst); ipsi O.* 34. *testimonii est inartificiale*] *Dyce (subst); testimonis est in arte fetialis O.* 36–7. argumentum / Cannot] *Broughton (subst);* argumentum cannot *O.* 38. SH. *Ramus.*] *Broughton (subst); Ra. O.* 42. writ] *O (wrote).* 44. contain] *Broughton (subst);* contains *O.*

---

32. *Excepting against*] i.e taking exception to, objecting to.

33. ipse dixi] 'I myself have said it' (Latin), a formulaic conclusion to an argument whose strength is based on the authority of the argument's writer or the authority of earlier writers.

quiddity] 'subtlety or nicety in argument; a quibble' (*OED*, n., 2a). See *Faustus*, A-text 1.1.166.

34. Argumentum testimonii est inartificiale] 'an argument from [the speaker's or writer's] authority is invalid' (Latin). Roland MacIlmaine translates Ramus's definition of the *inartificiale* argument in *Dialecticae Libri Duo* as follows: 'The argument unartificial or without art is an argument which proveth or disproveth not of his own nature but by the strength which it hath of some argument artificial and, therefore, when the matter is deeply considered, it hath but little strength to prove or disprove. In civil and temporal affairs, the authority of the disputer giveth no little credit thereunto if he be wise, virtuous, and have the benevolence of the auditor. All these by one name may be called a testimony' (Ramus [1574], 65).

36. nego argumentum] 'I deny the argument' (Latin).

41. *latter*] last.

purge myself] i.e. defend my reputation or, alternatively, cleanse my soul by confessing.

43. *Shekins*] Scheckius, Jacob Schegk (1511–87), a professor at the University of Tubingen who opposed Ramus's methodological innovations (Schmitt and Skinner, 836).

44. *places*] commonplaces or topics of argument.

SC. 9]   THE MASSACRE AT PARIS   81

 And I reduced it into better form,
 And this for Aristotle will I say,
 That he that despiseth him can ne'er
 Be good in logic or philosophy,
 And that's because the blockish Sorbonnists   50
 Attribute as much unto their works
 As to the service of the eternal God.
Guise. Why suffer you that peasant to declaim?
 Stab him, I say, and send him to his friends in hell.
Anjou. Ne'er was there collier's son so full of pride.   55

    [*He*] *kill*[*s*] *him.*

Guise. My lord of Anjou, there are a hundred Protestants
 Which we have chased into the river Seine
 That swim about and so preserve their lives.
 How may we do? I fear me they will live.
Dumaine. Go place some men upon the bridge   60
 With bows and darts to shoot at them they see
 And sink them in the river as they swim.

---

50. Sorbonnists] *Broughton (subst);* thorbonest *O.*   55.1. SD.] *printed on 55, aligned right, in O.*   57. Seine] *conj Malone, Broughton (subst);* Rene *O.*

---

 46. *reduced*] reorganised, condensed.
 50. *blockish*] stupid, unreceptive, stubborn.
 Sorbonnists] theologians of the Collège de Sorbonne, the University of Paris's major faculty of theology. The Sorbonnists were resolutely Catholic and Aristotelian.
 53. *declaim*] 'speak aloud with studied rhetorical force and expression; to make a speech on a set subject or theme as an exercise in public oratory or disputation' (*OED*, v., 1a).
 55. *collier's*] coal seller's, coal miner's (*OED*, n., 2a, 4). The author of *Rami vita* (1599) writes that 'Carbonarius pater probri loco illi objectus est [His father was accused of being a collier from a disreputable region]' but that in fact 'pater agricola fuit [his father was a farmer]' (qtd Dyce, 316). *OED* n.3 cites *Twelfth Night*, 3.4.116, 'What man, tis not for gravity to play at cherry-pit with Satan. Hang him, foul Collier', an insult, obviously, as colliers were proverbially associated with the devil.
 56–8.] Hotman records that 'common labourers and porters, and other of the most rascals of the peoples and desperate villains, to have the spoil of their clothes, stripped the dead bodies stark naked and threw them into the river of Seine' (*True and Plain Report*, lxii).
 61. *darts*] arrows.

Guise. 'Tis well advised, Dumaine. Go see it straight be
   done.
                              [*Exit* DUMAINE.]
And in the meantime, my lord, could we devise
To get those pedants from the King Navarre,   65
That are tutors to him and the Prince of Condé—
Anjou. For that let me alone. Cousin, stay you here,
And when you see me in then follow hard.

> *He knocketh, and enter the King of* NAVARRE *and*
> *Prince of* CONDÉ, *with their schoolmasters.*

How now, my lords, how fare you?
Navarre. My lord, they say that all the Protestants are
   massacred.   70
Anjou. Ay, so they are, but yet what remedy?
I have done what I could to stay this broil.
Navarre. But yet, my lord, the report doth run
That you were one that made this massacre.

63.1. SD.] *Dyce (subst); not in O.*   70. SH. *Navarre.*] *Ribner (subst);*
Nauar. O.   71. Ay] *Broughton (subst);* I *O.*   73. SH. *Navarre.*] *Ribner*
(subst); Nauarr. O.

---

65. *pedants*] tutors, teachers, schoolmasters (*OED*, n., 1).
67–8. *stay ... hard*] i.e. Anjou directs Guise to stay where he is on the main stage while Anjou moves up stage to the discovery space behind (see note 68 SD], and then follow him 'hard', forcefully, fiercely (*OED*, adv., 1).
68.1. SD.] The immediately preceding dialogue fluidly propels the action from one locale, Ramus's study, to the next location, presumably the Louvre, where Navarre was lodged. Mariko Ichikawa states that 'The stages of most London professional playhouses of the early modern period almost certainly had three doorways: a broad central opening and two flanking doorways ... [I]t is very likely that the central opening was fitted with double doors and the two flanking doorways had single doors' (72). The central opening might also have been curtained instead of having double doors. If the immediately preceding action has taken place at the front of the main stage, then Anjou might walk to the back of the stage and knock on the central tiring house façade door, from which Navarre and Condé then enter the stage.
72. *stay*] to appease, allay (strife, tumult); to reduce to order, bring under control (rebellious elements) (*OED*, v.1, 28, citing this example).
   broil] i.e. the commotion of the massacres.
74. *made*] brought about, caused to happen (*OED*, make, v.9).

SC. 9]   THE MASSACRE AT PARIS   83

Anjou. Who, I? You are deceived. I rose but now.   75
    [GUISE *follows* ANJOU *to the back of the stage.*]
Guise. Murder the Huguenots! Take those pedants hence.
Navarre. Thou traitor, Guise, lay off thy bloody hands.
Condé. Come, let us go tell the King.
                    [*Exeunt* NAVARRE *and* CONDÉ.]
Guise.   Come, sirs,
    I'll whip you to death with my poniard's point.
                He kills them.
Anjou. Away with them both.   *Exit* ANJOU.   80
Guise. And now, sirs, for this night let our fury stay;
    Yet will we not that the massacre shall end.
    Gonzague, post you to Orléans,

---

75. SH. *Anjou.*] Broughton; *An. O.*   75.1. SD] *this edn; Enter* Guise *O.*
77. SH. *Navarre.*] Ribner (subst); *Na. O.*   78. SH. *Condé.*] Ribner (subst); *Condy. O.*   78.1. SD. *Exeunt* NAVARRE *and* CONDÉ] Broughton (subst); *not in O.*   79.1. SD.] *printed on 79, aligned right, in O.*   80. SH. *Anjou.*] Broughton (subst); *An. O.*   83. Orléans] Broughton (subst); Orleance *O.*

75.1. SD.] O gives the stage direction '*Enter* Guise' here, but Anjou's internal SD at line 68 'when you see me in follow me hard' (67–8) suggests that now that Guise sees Anjou 'in' the scene with Navarre, Condé, and the schoolmasters, he follows Anjou's route to the back of the stage and 'enters' the newly established playing area representing Navarre's quarters.
    79. *poniard's*] sword's.
    81. *stay*] cease, stop. *OED*, v.23, d, 'to cause (a bell) to cease ringing. *Obsolete.*' This is the first usage cited.
    82–5.] Hotman narrates that 'This butcherly slaughter of Paris thus performed … immediately messengers were sent in post into all parts of the realm, with oft shifting their horses for haste, to command all other cities in the King's name to follow the example of Paris and to cause to be killed as many as they had among them of the reformed Religion' (*True and Plan Report*, lxiii).
    82. *will*] wish, desire, intend.
    83. *Orléans*] Historians estimate that between 150 and 500 Huguenots were massacred between 25 and 29 August 1572 in Orléans, which is 130 km south of Paris (Jouanna, 143).

Retz to Dieppe, Montsoreau unto Rouen,
And spare not one that you suspect of heresy.   85
And now stay that bell that to the devil's matins rings;
Now every man put off his burgonet
And so convey him closely to his bed.

Exeunt.

[SCENE 10]

Enter ANJOU, *with two* Lords of Poland.

Anjou. My lords of Poland, I must needs confess
   The offer of your Prince Electors far
   Beyond the reach of my deserts,
   For Poland is, as I have been informed,
   A martial people, worthy such a king   5
   As hath sufficient counsel in himself

---

84. Dieppe] *Broughton (subst);* Deep *O.*   Rouen] *Broughton (subst);* Roan *O.* 86. the] *Broughton (subst);* ye *O.*

Heading Sc. 10] *Bullen (subst); not in O.*

---

84. *Dieppe*] Although Hotman mentions Dieppe (*True and Plan Report,* lxxxvi), modern historians do not single it out as a focal point for the spread of anti-Huguenot violence into provincial France in the aftermath of the massacres in Paris.

   Rouen] Historians estimate that between 300 and 600 Huguenots were massacred between 17 and 20 September 1572 in Rouen, which is 110 km north-west of Paris (Jouanna, 143).

   86. *matins*] morning church service.
   88. *him*] himself.

[Historically, Anjou was proclaimed King of Poland on 11 May 1573 (Jouanna, 169). Two Polish ambassadors announced the news to Henry on 5 June 1573, while he was conducting the siege of La Rochelle, a Huguenot stronghold that had rebelled after the 1572 massacres (Solnon, 135). Poland's monarch was elected by its nobility, the 'prince electors' referred to in line 2 of the scene, and its throne had been vacant since the death of Sigismond Auguste II Jagelon on 7 July 1572 (Solnon, 123).]

   2. *Prince Electors*] Polish nobles who elected Henry as king. See headnote.
   3. *deserts*] deserving, merit, worth.
   5. *martial*] warlike. Situated on the frontiers of both Russia and the Ottoman Empire, the Poles were necessarily a 'martial people', if only because during the early modern period they were frequently the target of Russian and Ottoman imperial aggression. Greene's *Selimus* alludes to the

To lighten doubts and frustrate subtle foes
And such a king whom practice long hath taught
To please himself with manage of the wars,
The greatest wars within our Christian bounds, 10
I mean our wars against the Muscovites
And, on the other side, against the Turk,
Rich princes both and mighty emperors.
Yet by my brother Charles, our King of France,
And by His Grace's council, it is thought 15
That if I undertake to wear the crown
Of Poland, it may prejudice their hope
Of my inheritance to the crown of France,
For if th'Almighty take my brother hence,
By due descent the regal seat is mine. 20
With Poland therefore must I covenant thus:
That if by death of Charles the diadem
Of France be cast on me, then with your leaves
I may retire me to my native home.
If your commission serve to warrant this, 25
I thankfully shall undertake the charge
Of you and yours and carefully maintain
The wealth and safety of your kingdom's right.

Poles' reputation for martial valour when he refers to the 'Polonian' who 'comes hurtling in / Under the conduct of some foreign prince / To fight in honour of his crucifix' (*Selimus*, 4.11–13).

    9. *manage*] management. Apart from the use of this word again in this play, *OED*, v., 5a notes that Marlowe uses it in a military context in *1 Tamburlaine* (citing 3.1.34), and it also appears in *2 Tamburlaine*, 5.3.36.

    10. *Christian bounds*] the boundaries of Catholic Christendom, until the Protestant Reformation roughly coterminous with western Europe.

    11. *Muscovites*] Russians, who were Eastern Orthodox Christians. Ivan the Terrible (r. 1547–84) was Tsar of Russia at the time of this scene (Oliver, 121).

    12. *the Turk*] Emperor of the Ottoman Empire, which was Islamic. Selim II (r. 1566–74) was the Ottoman Emperor at the time of this scene.

    17. *prejudice*] impair, damage, affect unfavourably (*OED*, v., 1).

    21. *covenant*] make it a condition or clause of an agreement, stipulate (*OED*, v.3, citing this example).

    23. *leaves*] permission.

    25.] i.e. if the negotiating powers granted to you by your government permit you to assure me of this.

Lord. All this and more Your Highness shall command
   For Poland's crown and kingly diadem.   30
Anjou. Then come, my lords, let's go.
                                                       Exeunt.

[SCENE 11]

Enter two [1 Soldier and 2 Soldier] *with the*
ADMIRAL's *body.*

1 Soldier. Now, sirrah, what shall we do with the Admiral?
2 Soldier. Why, let us burn him for a heretic.
1 Soldier. Oh no. His body will infect the fire, and the fire the
   air, and so we shall be poisoned with him.
2 Soldier. What shall we do, then?   5
1 Soldier. Let's throw him into the river.
2 Soldier. Oh, 'twill corrupt the water, and the water the fish,
   and by the fish ourselves when we eat them.
1 Soldier. Then throw him into the ditch.
2 Soldier. No, no. To decide all doubts, be ruled by me: let's 10
   hang him here upon this tree.
1 Soldier. Agreed.

Heading Sc. 11] *Bullen (subst); not in O.*   1. SH. *1 Soldier.*] *this edn;* 1. *O.*
2. SH. *2 Soldier.*] *this edn;* 2. *O.*   2. a] *O (*an*).*   3. SH. *1 Soldier.*] *this edn;*
1. *O.*   5. SH. *2 Soldier.*] *this edn;* 2. *O.*   6. SH. *1 Soldier.*] *this edn;* 1. *O.*
7. SH. *2 Soldier.*] *this edn;* 2. *O.*   9. SH. *1 Soldier.*] *this edn;* 1. *O.*   10. SH.
2 Soldier.] *this edn;* 2. *O.*   12. SH. *1 Soldier.*] *this edn;* 1, *O.*   12.1. SD.] *printed
on 12, aligned right, in O.*

[Located at the gallows of Mount Faucon outside Paris. Hotman reports that after the Admiral had been murdered, defenestrated, trampled on, and mutilated, 'the common labourers and rascals three days together dragged the dead body, thus mangled and berayed with blood and filth, through the streets and afterward drew it out of town to the common gallows and hanged it up with a rope by the feet' (*True and Plain Report*, lvii). Later, 'the Queen mother, to feed her eyes with that spectacle, had a mind also to go thither, and she carried with her the King and both her other sons. But the next night following, the body was conveyed away and (as it is thought) buried' (*True and Plain Report*, lxxvii).]
   12.1. SD.] Elaborate apparatuses could be used on the Elizabethan stage to replicate hangings. In an undated entry between 3 October 1602 and 11 October 1602, Philip Henslowe, owner of the Rose theatre and manager of the Lord Admiral's Men, records payment of 14 pence 'for pulleys and

SC. 11]   THE MASSACRE AT PARIS   87

They hang him.

Enter the Duke of GUISE, *and* QUEEN MOTHER
[CATHERINE], *and the* CARDINAL.

Guise. Now, madam, how like you our lusty Admiral?
Catherine. Believe me, Guise, he becomes the place so well
    As I could long ere this have wished him there.   15
    But come, let's walk aside. Th'air's not very sweet.
Guise. No, by my faith, madam.
    Sirs, take him away and throw him in some ditch.
    [1 Soldier and 2 Soldier] *carry away the dead body.*
    And now, madam, as I understand,
    There are a hundred Huguenots and more   20
    Which in the woods do hold their synagogue
    And daily meet about this time of day,
    And thither will I to put them to the sword.
Catherine. Do so, sweet Guise. Let us delay no time,

---

24. SH. *Catherine.*] Ribner (subst); Qu. O.

workmanship for to hang Absolome' (Foakes, 217) in George Peele's biblical drama *David and Bathsheba*. However, if a dummy had been used for the Admiral's (headless and handless) body, the second soldier's 'let's hang him here upon this tree' (10–11) could suggest that either one of the stage pillars or a stage property representing a tree was used. Dessen and Thomson note that 'Trees are regularly cited in the dialogue (as when figures are tied to a tree) where a stage post may have been used' (236). In the 1587 edition of *Acts and Monuments*, Foxe records that the Admiral's body was hanged 'by the heels' (Foxe, 2153), and the acting company might plausibly have followed this widely known work's direction here.

13. *lusty*] lively, cheerful, handsome, gaily dressed (*OED*, adj., 1a, 2b).

14. *becomes*] suits.

21. *in the woods*] Hotman mentions that during the days of the massacre many Huguenots 'lurked some in the woods and some among their friends such as took pity on them' (*True and Plain Report*, lxxxv).

synagogue] religious meeting, 'an assembly: chiefly as a literalism of biblical translation' (*OED*, 4, citing this as example). 'Synagogue' narrowly denoted a Jewish religious meeting or meeting place, but Guise here applies it to the Huguenots' religious service in order to emphasise what he considers to be the Huguenots' heretical otherness to orthodox (Catholic) Christianity. The 1570 Edict of St Germain which ended the third War of Religion between French Catholics and the Huguenots granted Huguenots the liberty to worship outside city walls (Jouanna, 19).

24–7.] During the royal council on the eve before the massacre, Hotman records Catherine as arguing that 'if the Admiral recover his health all France will shortly be on fire with the fourth civil war' (*True and Plain Report*, l).

         For, if these stragglers gather head again   25
         And disperse themselves throughout the realm of
            France,
         It will be hard for us to work their deaths.
         Be gone, delay no time, sweet Guise.
Guise. Madam, I go as whirlwinds rage before a storm.
                                            Exit GUISE.
Catherine. My lord of Lorraine, have you marked of late   30
         How Charles our son begins for to lament
         For the late night's work which my lord of Guise
         Did make in Paris amongst the Huguenots?
Cardinal. Madam, I have heard him solemnly vow
         With the rebellious King of Navarre   35
         For to revenge their deaths upon us all.
Catherine. Ay, but, my lord, let me alone for that,
         For Catherine must have her will in France.
         As I do live, so surely shall he die,
         And Henry then shall wear the diadem;   40
         And if he grudge or cross his mother's will,
         I'll disinherit him and all the rest,
         For I'll rule France, but they shall wear the crown,
         And if they storm I then may pull them down.
         Come, my lord, let us go.   45
                                            Exeunt.

30. SH. *Catherine.*] *Ribner (subst);* Qu. O. 34. SH. *Cardinal.*] *Ribner (subst);* Card. O. 37. SH. *Catherine.*] *Ribner (subst);* Qu. O. 37. Ay] *Broughton (subst);* I O.

---

25. *stragglers*] See 4.2 and note.
   gather head] acquire strength (*OED*, gather v., 9).
   30-3.] According to Hotman, Charles's attitude in the days immediately after the massacre shifted from remorse to self-justification: 'the same King which but few days before by letters directed to all the governors of his provinces signified that his cousin the Admiral was slain by the Duke of Guise to his great sorrow and that himself was in great danger, the same King, I say, now caused it with sound of trumpet to be proclaimed that the traitorous and wicked Admiral was slain by his will and commandment' (*True and Plain Report*, lxxxvii). Other pamphlets suggested otherwise. See headnote to scene 13.
   30. *Lorraine*] Historically, Guise's ecclesiastical brother was the Cardinal of Guise; his uncle was the Cardinal of Lorraine.
   36. *For to*] to.
   39-40.] Catherine was suspected of poisoning Charles. See headnote to scene 13.
   44. *storm*] protest, resist.

[SCENE 12]

*Enter five or six Protestants with books, and [they]
kneel together. Enter also the* GUISE *[and others]*.

Guise. Down with the Huguenots! Murder them!
Protestant. O *Monsieur de Guise*, hear me but speak.
Guise. No, villain, that tongue of thine,
  That hath blasphemed the holy Church of Rome,
  Shall drive no plaints into the Guise's ears   5
  To make the justice of my heart relent.
  Tuez, tuez, tuez, let none escape!

  [The GUISE *and others] kill them [the Huguenots]*.

So, drag them away.
                                                      Exeunt.

[SCENE 13]

Enter the King of France [CHARLES], NAVARRE *and*
ÉPERNON *staying him[, and* PLESSIS]. *Enter* QUEEN
MOTHER [CATHERINE] *and the* CARDINAL.

Charles. Oh, let me stay and rest me here awhile.
  A gripping pain hath seized upon my heart,

Heading Sc. 12] *Bullen (subst); not in O.* 0.2. SD. *and others*] Broughton *(subst); not in O.* 7.1. SD. *kill them.*] *printed on 7, aligned right, in O.*

Heading Sc. 13] *Bullen (subst); not in O.* 0.2. SD. ÉPERNON] *O (*Epernoune*). Modernised silently throughout.* QUEEN] Broughton *(subst);* Qu. *O.* 1. SH. *Charles.*] Broughton *(subst); King. O.* 2. gripping] *O (*griping*)*.

[The 'woods' where the Huguenots 'do hold their synagogue' (11.21), to which Guise refers in the previous scene as his destination before exiting.]

5. *plaints*] laments, pleas, complaints, expressions of grievance (*OED*, n., 1a, 3).

[Charles died of tuberculosis on 30 May 1574. One of Marlowe's possible sources, Jean de Serres's *The Fourth Part of Commentaries of the Civil Wars in France* (1576), relates that 'it was vehemently suspected that he [Charles] was poisoned' (148), and Kocher notes that many pamphlets of the time pointed the finger at Catherine ('Contemporary Pamphlet Backgrounds', 166). At the end of the scene Marlowe adds Navarre's escape from Court, which historically did not occur until 1576.]

0. SD. *staying*] supporting.
1. *stay*] stop.

A sudden pang, the messenger of death.
Catherine. Oh, say not so. Thou killst thy mother's heart.
Charles. I must say so. Pain forceth me complain.   5
Navarre. Comfort yourself, my lord, and have no doubt
   But God will sure restore you to your health.
Charles. Oh no, my loving brother of Navarre.
   I have deserved a scourge, I must confess,
   Yet is there patience of another sort   10
   Than to misdo the welfare of their king.
   God grant my nearest friends may prove no worse.
   Oh, hold me up. My sight begins to fail,

---

4. SH. *Catherine.*] *Ribner (subst); Qu. O.*   5. SH. *Charles.*] *Broughton (subst); King. O.*   6. SH. *Navarre.*] *Ribner (subst); Na. O.*   8. SH. *Charles.*] *Broughton (subst); King. O.*   11. Than] *Broughton (subst);* Then *O.*

---

9. *scourge*] whip, whipping.

10–11.] i.e. the Huguenots' response to the massacre could have been other than to assassinate their king (which is what Charles seems to assume that they have done). The author of *Vindiciae contra Tyrannos* (1579), often considered to be French Huguenot Hubert Lanquet or Phillipe du Plessis-Mornay (Plessis in the play), argued that it was legitimate for subjects to assassinate tyrannical monarchs (monarchs who 'have deserved a scourge'). The work was initially published under the pseudonym 'Junius Brutus', one of Julius Caesar's assassins, and the author writes that 'as God doth oftentimes chastise a people by the cruelty of tyrants, so also doth He many times punish tyrants by the hands of the people' (*Vindiciae*, 132). The 'patience of another sort' that Charles would have preferred is presumably the passive suffering advocated in such works as the Elizabethan *An Homily Against Disobedience and Wilful Rebellion* (1570). The homily declares that 'kings and princes, as well the evil as the good, do reign by God's ordinance and that subjects are bounden to obey them' (A2^v). Charles's sentiments are, ironically, addressed to Navarre, who will profit from Charles's death and, later, Henri III's assassination. The historical irony of which Marlowe could not have been aware is, of course, that Navarre himself, as Henri IV, would be assassinated in 1610.

11. *misdo*] do harm or injury to (*OED*, v., 1).

12.] Suggesting that lines 9–12 'may be corrupt', Oliver glosses this line as follows: 'I pray that my nearest friends are of the better kind – and have not been responsible for my death' (126). Charles might cynically be suggesting that if it is in fact his 'nearest friends' who have assassinated him, then they, who have no cause to do so, are worse than his rebellious subjects, who arguably do have such cause ('I have deserved a scourge', Charles admits in line 9).

SC. 13]   THE MASSACRE AT PARIS   91

    My sinews shrink, my brains turn upside down,
    My heart doth break, I faint and die.   15
                He dies.
Catherine. What, art thou dead? Sweet son, speak to thy
        mother.
    Oh no, his soul is fled from out his breast,
    And he nor hears nor sees us what we do.
    My lords, what resteth there now for to be done
    But that we presently dispatch ambassadors   20
    To Poland to call Henry back again
    To wear his brother's crown and dignity.
    Épernon, go see it presently be done,
    And bid him come without delay to us.
Épernon. Madam, I will.   *Exit* ÉPERNON.   25
Catherine. And now, my lords, after these funerals be done,
    We will, with all the speed we can, provide
    For Henry's coronation from Poland.
    Come, let us take his body hence.
            All go out but NAVARRE *and* PLESSIS.
Navarre. And now, Navarre, whilst that these broils do last, 30
    My opportunity may serve me fit

15.1. SD.] *printed on 15, aligned right, in* O.   16. SH. *Catherine.*] *Ribner (subst);* Queene, O.   25. SH. *Épernon.*] *Ribner (subst);* Eper. O.   25. SD. ÉPERNON.] *Ribner (subst);* Eper. O.   28. Poland] *this edn;* Polonie O.   29.1. SD.] *centred* O.   PLESSIS] O *(*Pleshe*). Modernised silently throughout.*   30. SH. *Navarre.*] *Ribner (subst);* Nauar, O.

16.] The line echoes *The True Tragedy*, 'Ah Ned, speak to thy mother, boy' (sig. E5ʳ).
17. *his ... breast*] A common belief; see 'As virtuous men pass mildly away, / And whisper to their souls, to go / While some of their sad friends do say, / The breath goes now, and some say, no', Donne, 'A Valediction: Forbidding Mourning', 1–4.
18.] The line echoes *The True Tragedy*, 'And he nor sees nor hears us what we say' (sig. C4ʳ).
19. *resteth*] remains.
23. *Épernon*] Jean-Louis de la Valette (1554–1642), Henry's chief *mignon* along with Joyeuse. Henry elevated Valette to Duke of Épernon in 1581 (Solnon, 259–65).
31. *serve ... fit*] i.e. suit my purpose.

92   THE MASSACRE AT PARIS   [SC. 13

    To steal from France and hie me to my home.
    For here's no safety in the realm for me,
    And, now that Henry is called from Poland,
    It is my due by just succession.   35
    And therefore, as speedily as I can perform,
    I'll muster up an army secretly,
    For fear that Guise, joined with the King of Spain,
    Might seem to cross me in mine enterprise.
    But God, that always doth defend the right,   40
    Will show His mercy and preserve us still.
Plessis. The virtues of our true religion
    Cannot but march with many graces more,
    Whose army shall discomfort all your foes
    And, at the length, in Pampelonia crown,   45
    In spite of Spain and all the popish power
    That holds it from Your Highness wrongfully,
    Your Majesty her rightful lord and sovereign.
Navarre. Truth, Plessis, and God so prosper me in all
    As I intend to labour for the truth   50
    And true profession of His holy Word.
    Come, Plessis, let's away whilst time doth serve.
    Exeunt.

38. King] *Broughton (subst);* K. *O.*   49. SH. *Navarre.*] *Ribner (subst); Nauar. O.*   52. SD. Exeunt] *Broughton (subst); Ezeunt O.*

---

    32. *steal*] depart secretly (*OED*, v.9a).
    hie me] go, hasten, speed; *OED* cites *Romeo and Juliet*, 3.2.138, 'Hie to your chamber'. After numerous attempts to escape the Court, where he had been confined and kept under surveillance since the Paris massacres, Navarre escaped Paris on 3 February 1576. His companion was not du Plessis but Agrippa d'Aubigné, another notable French poet (Seward, 46–7).
    34–5.] Although Henry's younger brother Alençon is still alive, the play makes Navarre the next in line to the French throne after Henry.
    37.] Having fled Paris, Navarre joined with the forces of Alençon and Condé in rebellion against Henry III in the last stages of the fifth War of Religion (1574–76). The war was concluded by an accord signed at Beaulieu, by which Navarre became governor of Guyenne (Garrisson, *Guerre civile*, 184–6).
    38. *King of Spain*] Philip II (r. 1556–98).
    39. *seem*] think fit (Oliver, 127; *OED*, v.2, 9b).
    42. SH. Plessis] Philippe de Mornay (1549–1623), Seigneur du Plessis Marly, one of Henry's chief advisors and a poet. Du Plessis visited England in 1577 and 1580, meeting Sir Philip Sidney and his sister Mary, who translated du Plessis's *Excellent discours de la vie et de la mort* (1577).
    45. *Pampelonia*] Pamplona was the capital city of Iberian Navarre (Navarre south of the Pyrenees), which was annexed by Spain in 1512.

[SCENE 14]

Sound trumpets within, and then all cry 'Vive le Roi!' *two or three times.*

Enter HENRY *crowned*, QUEEN [CATHERINE], CARDINAL, *Duke of* GUISE, ÉPERNON, *the King's minions* [*including* MAUGIRON], *with others, and the* Cutpurse.

All. Vive le Roi! Vive le Roi!

Sound trumpets.

Catherine. Welcome from Poland, Henry, once again,
Welcome to France, thy father's royal seat.
Here hast thou a country void of fears,
A warlike people to maintain thy right,   5
A watchful senate for ordaining laws,
A loving mother to preserve thy state,
And all things that a king may wish besides.
All this and more hath Henry with his crown.

Heading Sc. 14] *Bullen (subst); not in* O.   0.1. SD. 'Vive le Roi!'] *Broughton (subst);* viue la Roy O.   0.2. SD. ÉPERNON] O *(*Epernoone*). Modernised silently throughout.*   1. *le Roi*] *Broughton (subst);* la Roy O.   1.1. SD.] *printed on 1, aligned right, in* O.   2. SH. *Catherine.*] *Ribner (subst);* Qu. O.

[Anjou was crowned Henry III on 13 February 1575 at the Cathedral of Reims. The Cardinal of Guise officiated the coronation, and Guise and de Mayenne played important roles in the ceremony. Hostile observers commented on Henry's childish and frivolous behaviour during the proceedings. In his *La vie et faits notables de Henri de Valois* (1589), for example, Jean Boucher remarks that 'when the most noble Cardinal de Guise ... had anointed him and placed the crown of Charlemagne on his head, he cried quite loudly that it hurt him; and as the ceremonies of anointing and crowning were being celebrated, and as he looked at his minions here and there, making some inappropriate and petulant gestures that demonstrated his vanity, the crown twice slipped off his head and would have fallen to the ground, if an official nearby had not prevented it' (qtd Thomas and Tydeman, 279). The incident with the cutpurse dramatised by this scene does not occur in Marlowe's sources, but an analogue for it can be found in Sir Nicholas L'Estrange's manuscript collection of oral tales and jests compiled in the mid-seventeenth century (Bennett, 217).]

0.1. SD. Vive le Roi!] 'Long live the King!' (French).
0.3. SD. minions] favourites. See note to line 45 below.
6. *senate*] parliament.
7. *state*] throne, sovereignty, kingdom.

Cardinal. And long may Henry enjoy all this and more. 10
All. Vive le Roi! Vive le Roi!

     Sound trumpets.

Henry. Thanks to you all. The guider of all crowns
 Grant that our deeds may well deserve your loves,
 And so they shall, if fortune speed my will
 And yield your thoughts to height of my deserts. 15
 What say our minions? Think they Henry's heart
 Will not both harbour love and majesty?
 Put off that fear. They are already joined.
 No person, place, or time, or circumstance
 Shall slack my love's affection from his bent; 20
 As now you are, so shall you still persist,
 Removeless from the favours of your king.
Maugiron. We know that noble minds change not their thoughts
 For wearing of a crown, in that Your Grace
 Hath worn the Poland diadem before 25

---

10. SH. *Cardinal.*] *Ribner (subst); Car. O.* 10. and more] *Broughton (subst);* & more *O.* 11. *le Roi*] *Broughton (subst);* la Roy *O.* 11.1. SD.] *printed on 11, aligned right, in O.* 12. SH. *Henry.*] *Dyce (subst); Henry, O.* 16. say] *Broughton (subst);* saies *O.* 23. SH. *Maugiron*] *O (Mugeroun). Modernised silently throughout.*

 12. *guider ... crowns*] i.e. God.
 14–15. *if ... deserts*] i.e. if fortune helps my wish by matching your thoughts to my merits.
 14. *speed*] carry out (*OED*, v.8).
 20. *slack*] make lax, neglectful, or remiss (*OED*, v., 4).
 bent] inclination, tendency, propensity (*OED*, n.2, 6a). *OED*, n.2, 7 suggests 'That towards which an action, etc. is directed; aim, purpose, intention.'
 21. *persist*] to continue firmly despite opposition (*OED*, v., 1a).
 22. *Removeless*] that cannot be removed, unyielding, constant (*OED*, adj., citing this instance).
 23. SH. *Maugiron*] The play conflates two of Henry's *mignons*, Paul de Stuer de Caussade, sieur de Saint-Mégrin, and Louis de Maugiron. The former was suspected of being the Duchess of Guise's lover and in 1578 was beaten to death by a gang led by Guise's brother, the Duke of Mayenne. In the same year the latter was killed in a group duel that pitted three of Henry's *mignons* against three Guisians (Carroll, 235–6).

You were invested in the crown of France.
Henry. I tell thee, Maugiron, we will be friends,
    And fellows too, whatever storms arise.
Maugiron. Then may it please Your Majesty to give me leave
    To punish those that do profane this holy feast. 30

He cuts off the Cutpurse['s] *ear, for cutting of the gold buttons off his cloak.*

Henry. How meanst thou that?
Cutpurse. O Lord, mine ear!
Maugiron. Come, sir, give me my buttons, and here's your ear.
Guise. [*To an attendant*] Sirrah, take him away.
Henry. [*To the attendant*] Hands off, good fellow. I will be his bail 35
    For this offence. [*To the Cutpurse*] Go, sirrah, work no more
    Till this our coronation day be past.
    [*To the main group*] And now our solemn rites of coronation done,
    What now remains but for a while to feast
    And spend some days in barriers, tourney, tilt, 40
    And like disports, such as do fit the court?
    Let's go, my lords, our dinner stays for us.
            Go out all but the QUEEN [CATHERINE]
                and the CARDINAL.
Catherine. My Lord Cardinal of Lorraine, tell me,
    How likes Your Grace my son's pleasantness?

42.1. SD.] *centred* O.

26. *invested in*] established in the office of, installed (*OED*, v.5).
37. *coronation day*] Henry was crowned at Reims on 13 February 1575 (Solnon, 413).
40. *barriers, tourney, tilt*] fighting with swords across a barrier, chivalric tournament, and jousting.
41. *disports*] games, sports.
    do fit] are appropriate to.
44–6.] The lines echo Isabella's contemptuous remark to Lancaster about Edward's impatience for Gaveston's return from Ireland in *Edward the Second*: 'Look, Lancaster, how passionate he is, / And still his mind runs on his minion' (6.3–4).
44. *pleasantness*] pleasure-seeking nature.

His mind, you see, runs on his minions, 45
And all his heaven is to delight himself,
And, whilst he sleeps securely thus in ease,
Thy brother Guise and we may now provide
To plant ourselves with such authority
As not a man may live without our leaves. 50
Then shall the Catholic faith of Rome
Flourish in France, and none deny the same.
Cardinal. Madam, as in secrecy I was told,
My brother Guise hath gathered a power of men,
Which, as he saith, to kill the Puritans, 55
But 'tis the house of Bourbon that he means.
Now, madam, must you insinuate with the King
And tell him that 'tis for his country's good
And common profit of religion.
Catherine. Tush, man, let me alone with him 60
To work the way to bring this thing to pass,
And, if he do deny what I do say,
I'll dispatch him with his brother presently,
And then shall Monsieur wear the diadem.
Tush, all shall die unless I have my will, 65
For while she lives Catherine will be Queen.

---

53. SH. *Cardinal.*] Ribner *(subst); Car. O.* 60. SH. *Catherine.*] Ribner *(subst); Qu. O.* 67. lord] Broughton *(subst);* Lords *O.*

49. *plant*] establish.

54. *power of men*] army. After forming the Holy League in 1584, Guise maintained a standing army funded by Spanish money. After the Treaty of Beaulieu in 1576, however, Guise and others had made an earlier attempt to form a Catholic League to oppose Protestantism and Navarre (Garrisson, *Guerre civile*, 114–18).

55. *Puritans*] Protestants, the more radical of whom in Elizabethan England had become known as 'Puritans' because of their desire to purge the Elizabethan Church of its supposed Catholic impurities.

56. *Bourbon*] Navarre belonged to the royal house of Bourbon.

57. *insinuate ... King*] i.e. work your way into the King's affection and thought.

64. *Monsieur*] François, Duke of Alençon, Henry's younger brother, whose existence is ignored by the rest of the play. Alençon died in 1584.

Come, my lord, let us go seek the Guise
And then determine of this enterprise.
Exeunt.

[SCENE 15]

Enter the DUCHESS *of Guise and her* Maid.

Duchess. Go, fetch me pen and ink—
Maid.   I will, madam.
                                            Exit Maid.
Duchess. That I may write unto my dearest lord.
   Sweet Maugiron, 'tis he that hath my heart,
   And Guise usurps it, 'cause I am his wife.
   Fain would I find some means to speak with him,   5
   But cannot, and therefore am enforced to write,

Heading Sc. 15] *Bullen (subst); not in* O.   1. SH. *Duchess.*] *Ribner (subst);*
Duch. O.   2. SH. *Duchess.*] *Ribner (subst); Duch.* O.   3. Maugiron] O
*(*Mugeroune*). Modernised silently throughout.*

---

   67. *lord*] Although O has 'lords', 42.1 SD makes it clear that at this point
only one lord, the Cardinal of Lorraine, remains on stage for Catherine to
address.
   [Although historically the confrontation between the Duchess and Guise
dramatised in this scene must have occurred before the deaths of the two
mignons conflated in the character of Maugiron in 1578 (see note to 14.23),
the play pushes it forward roughly a decade in order to incorporate the affair
into the events surrounding the Battle of Coutras (20 October 1587), with
which scenes 15-17 are concerned. No direct source available to Marlowe
has been found for the play's dramatisation of the affair (Kocher,
'Contemporary Pamphlet Backgrounds', 169; Thomas and Tydeman, 257).
Nonetheless, Kocher declares that 'I am convinced that Marlowe had some
contemporary account in front of him' ('Contemporary Pamphlet
Backgrounds', 169) and suggests an unknown earlier version of the account
published in 1609 in Jacques-Auguste de Thou's *Histoire Universelle.*]
   1. SH. Duchess] Catherine de Clèves (1548-1633), Countess of Eu, to
whom Guise was married in 1570 in order to put an end to his affair with
Margaret (Carroll, 189-90).
   3-4.] These lines echo *Arden of Faversham*, 1.1.98-100: 'Sweet Mosby is
the man that hath my heart, / And he usurps it, having nought but this— /
That I am tied to him by marriage.'
   5. *Fain ... I*] i.e. I would like to.

That he may come and meet me in some place
Where we may one enjoy the other's sight.

Enter the Maid *with [pen,] ink and paper.*

So, set it down, and leave me to myself.
[*Exit* Maid.]

She writes.

Oh, would to God this quill that here doth write 10
Had late been plucked from out fair Cupid's wing,
That it might print these lines within his heart.

Enter the GUISE.

Guise. What, all alone, my love, and writing too?
I prithee say to whom thou write.
Duchess. To such a one, my lord, as, when she reads my 15
lines,
Will laugh, I fear me, at their good array.
Guise. I pray thee let me see.
Duchess. Oh no, my lord, a woman only must
Partake the secrets of my heart.
Guise. But, madam, I must see. 20

He takes it.

8.1. SD. *pen*] *Oliver (subst); not in* O.   9.1. SD.] *Broughton (subst); not in* O.   9.2. SD.] *printed on 10, aligned left, in* O.   14. write] *this edn;* writes O.   15. SH. *Duchess.*] *Ribner (subst);* Duch. O.   15–16. lines, / Will] *Broughton (subst);* lines, will O.   18. SH. *Duchess.*] *Ribner (subst);* Duch. O.   18–19. must / Partake] *Broughton (subst);* must partake O.   20.1. SD.] *printed on 20, aligned right, in* O.

10–13.] The notion of extreme emotions being written on the heart may derive from Proverbs 3.3: 'Let not steadfast love and faithfulness forsake you; bind them around your neck; write them on the tablet of your heart.' The image of inscribing words on the heart is found in Ford's *Love's Sacrifice*: 'When I am dead, rip up my heart and read / With constant heart what now my tongue defines: / Fernando's name, carved out in bloody lines' (2.4.93–5).
14. *prithee*] pray thee.
16. *array*] arrangement, order, form.

Are these your secrets that no man must know?
Duchess. Oh, pardon me, my lord.
Guise. Thou trothless and unjust, what lines are these?
    Am I grown old, or is thy lust grown young,
    Or hath my love been so obscured in thee 25
    That others need to comment on my text?
    Is all my love forgot which held thee dear,
    Ay, dearer than the apple of mine eye?
    Is Guise's glory but a cloudy mist
    In sight and judgement of thy lustful eye? 30
    Mort dieu! Were't not the fruit within thy womb,
    Of whose increase I set some longing hope,
    This wrathful hand should strike thee to the heart.
    Hence, strumpet, hide thy head for shame,
    And fly my presence if thou look to live. 35
                             Exit [DUCHESS].
    O wicked sex, perjured and unjust!
    Now do I see that from the very first
    Her eyes and looks sowed seeds of perjury,
    But villain he to whom these lines should go
    Shall buy her love even with his dearest blood.   *Exit.* 40

---

22. SH. Duchess.] *Ribner (subst);* Duch. *O.*   26. need] *Broughton (subst);* needs *O.*   28. Ay] *Broughton (subst);* I *O.*   than] *Broughton (subst);* then *O.*   31. Mort dieu] *Broughton (subst);* Mor du *O.*   Were't] *Oliver (subst);* wert *O.*

---

  23. *trothless*] faithless, untrue, disloyal, untrustworthy (*OED* cites this example).
  unjust] lacking integrity or moral rectitude, wicked, sinful, dishonourable (*OED*, adj., 2, citing this instance).
  25–6.] Guise compares his love to an illegible word for which other pens supply substitutes by overwriting or commenting upon his text (his wife).
  31. Mort dieu] 'Death of God' (French).
  fruit] embryo.
  34. *strumpet*] whore.
  36. *wicked sex*] i.e. womankind.
  39. *villain he*] that villain.

[SCENE 16]

Enter the King of NAVARRE, PLESSIS *and* BARTAS, *and their train, with drums and trumpets.*

Navarre. My lords, since in a quarrel just and right
  We undertake to manage these our wars
  Against the proud disturbers of the faith—
  I mean the Guise, the Pope, and King of Spain—
  Who set themselves to tread us underfoot   5
  And rent our true religion from this land
  (But for you know our quarrel is no more
  But to defend their strange inventions
  Which they will put us to with sword and fire),
  We must with resolute minds resolve to fight   10
  In honour of our God and country's good.
  Spain is the council chamber of the Pope,
  Spain is the place where he makes peace and war,

Heading Sc. 16] *Bullen (subst); not in O.* 0.1. SD. BARTAS] *O (*Bartus*).* *Modernised silently throughout.* 1. since] *O (*sith*).* 6–7. land / (But] *Oliver (subst);* land. / But *O.* 9–10. fire), / We] *Bullen (subst);* fire: / We *O;* fire)— / We *Oliver (subst).*

[This scene takes place immediately before the Battle of Coutras in 1587, one of the crucial battles of the eighth War of Religion. Navarre and Condé led the Protestant forces, while the King, seconded by Guise and the Duke of Joyeuse, led the Catholic armies. On 20 October 1587, Navarre's army engaged and defeated the forces led by Joyeuse at Coutras, in south-western France.]

  3. *the faith*] i.e. Protestantism.
  proud disturber] In his edition of Marlowe's *Edward II*, Forker notes that this phrase is used in that play at 2.5.9, and in *The Troublesome Reign of King John* and *Edward I*.
  4. *Pope*] Pope Sixtus V (1585–90).
  6. *rent*] rend, tear.
  7. *But for*] but, since.
  8. *But*] than.
  defend] defend against, ward off, repel (*OED*, v., 6a).
  strange] extreme (*OED*, adj., 9a, 10a).
  inventions] plots, plans, new methods or means of doing something (*OED*, n., 3, 9).
  9. *put us to*] i.e. subject us to, inflict on us.

SC. 16]   THE MASSACRE AT PARIS   101

    And Guise for Spain hath now incensed the King
    To send his power to meet us in the field.   15
Bartas. Then in this bloody brunt they may behold
    The sole endeavour of your princely care:
    To plant the true succession of the faith
    In spite of Spain and all his heresies.
Navarre. The power of vengeance now encamps itself   20
    Upon the haughty mountains of my breast,
    Plays with her gory colours of revenge,
    Whom I respect as leaves of boasting green
    That change their colour when the winter comes,
    When I shall vaunt as victor in revenge.   25

---

14. *for*] i.e. at Spain's instigation, on Spain's behalf.
incensed] inspired, spurred, moved.
15. *power*] army (*OED*, n.1, 7a).
16. SH. Bartas] Guillaume de Salluste (1544–90), Seigneur du Bartas, Huguenot courtier and poet, best known in England for his epic rendition of biblical history in *La Sepmaine; ou Creation du Monde* (1578) and *La Seconde Semaine* (1584–1603).
16. *brunt*] 'assault, charge, onset, violent attack' (*OED*, n.1, 2). See 'stranger engines for the brunt of war', *Doctor Faustus*, A-text, 1.1.97.
18. *true ... faith*] i.e. Protestantism, which, according to Protestants, had returned to the true roots of Christianity.
20–5.] The figurative language of these lines is strained and open to multiple interpretations. The 'power of vengeance' in line 20 most obviously refers to Navarre's army, currently 'encamped' in the environs of Coutras before the upcoming battle. In line 21, Navarre figures his 'breast' as the site of his army's encampment: in the terms of his metaphor, his desire for revenge is mountainous, adequately represented or expressed only by the military force of his army. In the following line, Navarre genders the army (the 'power of vengeance', which is the main grammatical subject of these lines) feminine, suggesting a personification of it as the goddess Revenge. This personification is strengthened by his figuration of his soldiers' unfurling of their ensigns as '[p]lay[ing] with her gory colours of revenge'. Lines 22–3 compare the 'colours of revenge' to the changing colours of leaves, which are initially green but acquire more ominous hues, such as orange and red, when they die and fall in the winter. Anticipating victory in his upcoming battle with the King's forces, Navarre suggests that although now his 'power' or army might seem 'green', it will appear violent and bloody as soldiers fall on the battlefield.
21. *haughty*] high, proud.
22. *colours*] flags, ensigns.
23. *respect*] regard, look upon (*OED*, v., 3d, second cited use).
25. *vaunt*] boast.

Enter a Messenger.

How now, sirrah, what news?
Messenger. My lord, as by our scouts we understand,
A mighty army comes from France with speed,
Which is already mustered in the land
And means to meet Your Highness in the field. 30
Navarre. In God's name, let them come.
This is the Guise that hath incensed the King
To levy arms and make these civil broils.
But canst thou tell who is their general?
Messenger. Not yet, my lord, for thereon do they stay, 35
But, as report doth go, the Duke of Joyeuse
Hath made great suit unto the King therfore.
Navarre. It will not countervail his pains, I hope.
I would the Guise in his stead might have come,
But he doth lurk within his drousy couch 40
And makes his footstool on security.
So he be safe he cares not what becomes
Of king or country, no not for them both.
But come, my lords, let us away with speed
And place ourselves in order for the fight. 45
Exeunt.

---

27. SH. *Messenger.*] Ribner (subst); *Mes. O.*   29. is] Broughton (subst); are *O.*   31. SH. *Navarre.*] Ribner (subst); *Na. O.*   35. SH. *Messenger.*] Ribner (subst); *Mes. O.*   36. Joyeuse] *O* (Ioyeux). *Modernised silently throughout.*   38. SH. *Navarre.*] Ribner (subst); *Na. O.*

---

35. thereon ... stay] i.e. they have yet to decide upon that.
36. *Duke of Joyeuse*] Anne de Joyeuse (1560-87), Henry's chief *mignon* along with Épernon. Baron d'Arques, he was elevated to Duke in 1581 (Solnon, 259–65).
37. *therfore*] for it.
38. *It*] i.e. the rewards of the generalship or rank of general.
countervail] counterbalance, equal, match.
41.] The line echoes *The True Tragedy*, 'And made our footstool of security' (sig. E6ᵛ).

[SCENE 17]

Enter the King of France [HENRY], *Duke of* GUISE,
ÉPERNON, *and* Duke JOYEUSE.

Henry. My sweet Joyeuse, I make thee general
Of all my army now in readiness
To march against the rebellious King Navarre.
At thy request I am content thou go,
Although my love to thee can hardly suffer, 5
Regarding still the danger of thy life.
Joyeuse. Thanks to Your Majesty, and so I take my leave.
Farewell to my lord of Guise and Épernon.
Guise. Health and hearty farewell to my lord Joyeuse.
                                        Exit JOYEUSE.
Henry. So kindly, cousin of Guise, you and your wife 10
Do both salute our lovely minions.

Heading Sc. 17] *Bullen (subst); not in O.* 1. SH. *Henry.*] *Dyce (subst);*
King. O. 10. SH. *Henry.*] *Dyce (subst); King. O.* 10–11. wife /
Do] *Broughton (subst);* wife doe *O.* 11.1. SD.] *aligned right O.*

[After sending Joyeuse to his imminent doom at Coutras, the scene returns the play's attention to the conflict between Guise and Henry's *mignons*. Henry's taunting of Guise is consonant with de Thou's assertion that Henry 'believed himself well avenged for the humiliations he had received from him [Guise], by the revenge which St-Mégrin took in dishonouring him, and by the jokes he himself made about this affair, when he was with his favourites' (*Histoire universelle*, qtd Thomas and Tydeman, 282). De Thou also relates that once Henry learned of the plans made to assassinate St-Mégrin he attempted to persuade his *mignon* to be careful, but 'the monarch's entreaties, instead of weakening the young lord's naturally high mettle, which was made yet prouder by the king's favour, served only to provoke him further to despise the danger and to run to his doom' (qtd Thomas and Tydeman, 282).]
3. *rebellious*] In 1585 Pope Sixtus V issued a papal bull excommunicating Navarre and stripping him of his royal status. Although Henry III rejected the papal interference in the matter of the succession to the French crown and refused to allow the bull to be published in France, he declared anyone who took arms against the forces of the Catholic League to be guilty of treason (Pitts, 115).
5. *suffer*] suffer it, bear it, endure it.
6. *Regarding still*] always considering, heeding.
11. SD. makes horns] places his index fingers to his forehead like horns, a contemptuous gesture intended to taunt Guise for his wife's infidelity.

He makes horns at the GUISE.

Remember you the letter, gentle sir,
Which your wife wrote to my dear minion
And her chosen friend?
Guise. How now, my lord? Faith, this is more than need! 15
Am I thus to be jested at and scorned?
'Tis more than kingly or imperious,
And sure if all the proudest kings in
Christendom should bear me such derision,
They should know how I scorned them and their 20
    mocks.
I love your minions? Dote on them yourself!
I know none else but holds them in disgrace,
And here by all the saints in heaven I swear,
That villain for whom I bear this deep disgrace,
Even for your words that have incensed me so, 25
Shall buy that strumpet's favour with his blood
Whether he have dishonoured me or no.
Par la mort dieu, il mourra!   *Exit.*
Henry. Believe me, this jest bites sore.
Épernon. My lord, 'twere good to make them friends, 30
For his oaths are seldom spent in vain.

12–14. sir, / Which ... minion / And] *Oliver (subst);* sir, which ... Minion, and *O.* 13. wrote] *O (writ).* 15. than] *Broughton (subst);* then *O.* 17. than] *Broughton (subst);* then *O.* 28. Par ... mourra] *Broughton (subst); Par la mor du, il mora O.* 29. SH. Henry.] *Dyce (subst);* King. *O.* 30. SH. Épernon.] *Ribner (subst);* Eper, *O.*

---

15. *Faith*] truly; a mild oath.
    need] necessary.
17. *imperious*] imperial.
19. *bear ... derision*] i.e. mock me in this fashion.
20. *mocks*] derisive comments or acts.
22. *disgrace*] (public) disfavour.
24. *disgrace*] affront to personal honour.
28. Par ... mourra] 'By the death of God, he will die' (French).

Enter MAUGIRON.

Henry. How now, Maugiron, metst thou not the Guise at
  the door?
Maugiron. Not I, my lord. What if I had?
Henry. Marry, if thou hadst thou mightst have had the stab,
  For he hath solemnly sworn thy death. 35
Maugiron. I may be stabbed and live till he be dead.
  But wherefore bears he me such deadly hate?
Henry. Because his wife bears thee such kindly love.
Maugiron. If that be all, the next time that I meet her
  I'll make her shake off love with her heels. 40
  But which way is he gone? I'll go make a walk
  On purpose from the court to meet with him. *Exit.*
Henry. I like not this. Come, Épernon,
  Let's go seek the Duke and make them friends.
                                                    Exeunt.

---

32. SH. *Henry.*] *Dyce (subst); King. O.* 33. SH. *Maugiron.*] *Ribner (subst); Muge. O.* 34. SH. *Henry.*] *Dyce (subst); King. O.* 36. SH. *Maugiron.*] *Ribner (subst); Muge. O.* 38. SH. *Henry.*] *Dyce (subst); King. O.* 39. SH. *Maugiron.*] *Ribner (subst); Muge. O.* 41–2. walk / On] *Dyce (subst);* walk on *O.* 43. SH. *Henry.*] *Dyce (subst); King. O.* 43–4. Épernon, / Let's] *Dyce (subst); Epernoune* lets *O.*

34. *Marry*] variant of 'Mary', used as an interjection for emphasis (*OED*, int.).
  the stab] death by stabbing (*OED*, n.1, 2c).
36. *I may ... dead*] i.e. If Guise assaults me, he will be the one who dies in the fight.
38. *bears ... love*] i.e. she loves Maugiron; she bears his weight when the two are making love.
40. *shake ... heels*] i.e. to satisfy her sexual desire by moving her body. See 'With hey, trixy, terely-whiskin, / The world it runs on wheels. / When the young man's ————, / Up goes the maiden's heels' (Beaumont, *The Knight of the Burning Pestle*, 5.5.199–201). Oliver comments that '"make" suggests the deliberateness of the decision' (138).

[SCENE 18]

Alarms within. The Duke JOYEUSE *slain.*

Enter the King of NAVARRE *and his train* [BARTAS *and others*].

Navarre. The Duke is slain and all his power dispersed,
   And we are graced with wreaths of victory.
   Thus God, we see, doth ever guide the right,
   To make His glory great upon the earth.
Bartas. The terror of this happy victory, 5
   I hope, will make the King surcease his hate
   And either never manage army more
   Or else employ them in some better cause.
Navarre. How many noblemen have lost their lives
   In prosecution of these cruel arms 10
   Is ruth and almost death to call to mind,
   But God, we know, will always put them down
   That lift themselves against the perfect truth,
   Which I'll maintain so long as life doth last

Heading Sc. 18] *Bullen (subst); not in O.* 5. SH. Bartas.] *Ribner (subst); Bar. O.* 9. SH. Navarre.] *Ribner (subst); Na. O.*

[The aftermath of the Battle of Coutras.]
 0.1. SD. Alarms] the sounding of drums or trumpets to signal the onset of attack.
 The Duke JOYEUSE slain] Joyeuse was shot and killed as he tried to surrender (Pitts, 128). Oliver interprets this stage direction as an offstage shout, '*The* Duke Joyeux [is] slain' (xviii.0.1 s.d.), eliminating any stage action preceding the entrance of Navarre and his entourage. The octavo stage direction, however, retained here, clearly suggests the inclusion of a brief dumb show in which the Duke is killed in battle.
 0.2. SD. train] retinue.
 2.] The line repeats *The True Tragedy*, 'and we are graced with wreaths of victory' (sig. C4ʳ). In *3 Henry VI*, the line is moved to 5.3.2.
 6. *surcease*] leave off, stop, desist, cease (*OED*, v., 1)
 10. *prosecution ... arms*] i.e. the conduct of these cruel wars.
 11. *ruth*] matter for or occasion of sorrow or regret (*OED*, n., 3a).

And with the Queen of England join my force 15
To beat the papal monarch from our lands
And keep those relics from our countries' coasts.
Come, my lords, now that this storm is overpast,
Let us away with triumph to our tents.

Exeunt.

[SCENE 19]

Enter a Soldier.

Soldier. Sir, to you, sir, that dares make the Duke a cuckold and use a counterfeit key to his privy chamber door! And although you take out nothing but your own, yet you put in that which displeaseth him and so forestall his market and set up your standing where you should not. And 5 whereas he is your landlord, you will take upon you to be his and till the ground that he himself should occupy,

---

15. Queen] *Broughton (subst);* Q. *O.* 17. countries'] *Broughton (subst);* countries *O.*

Heading Sc. 19] *Bullen (subst); not in O.* 1. SH. *Soldier.*] *Broughton (subst); Soul. O.* 1. cuckold and] *Broughton (subst);* cuckolde, / And *O.*

---

15. *Queen of England*] Queen Elizabeth I (r. 1558–1603), who had been giving the French Huguenot forces limited support with money and troops since 1562, and lent Navarre and Condé 300,000 livres in 1586 (Garrisson, *Guerre civile,* 52–3, 198).
16. *papal monarch*] Pope.
17. *our countries'*] England's and France's.

[Paris. Historically, Guise's brother the Duke of Mayenne arranged the murder of St-Mégrin (see note to 14.23), apparently, according to de Thou, because Guise himself 'was too occupied by important projects to give the matter the slightest attention' (*Histoire universelle,* qtd Thomas and Tydeman, 282). The scene segues from the murder to the Day of Barricades in May 1588.]

1. *cuckold*] man whose wife is having sex with another man.
2. *counterfeit*] copied, duplicated without authority. Maugiron may literally possess a duplicate of the key to Guise's bedroom ('privy chamber'), but the key is also a metaphor for his penis.

privy chamber] bedroom; his wife's private parts.
4. *forestall*] pre-empt.
5. *standing*] market booth; erect penis.
7. *occupy*] possess; have sexual intercourse with.

which is his own free land—if it be not too free: there's
the question. And, though I come not to take possession
(as I would I might), yet I mean to keep you out, which   10
I will if this gear hold. What, are ye come so soon? Have
at ye, sir.

Enter MAUGIRON.

He [the Soldier] *shoots at him* [MAUGIRON] *and kills him.*

Enter the GUISE *[and* Attendants].

Guise. Hold thee, tall soldier. [*Gives him money*] Take thee
this and fly.

Exit Soldier.

Lie there, the King's delight and Guise's scorn.
Revenge it, Henry, as thou list or dare: 15
I did it only in despite of thee.

[*The* Attendants] *take him* [MAUGIRON] *away.*

Enter the King [HENRY] *and* ÉPERNON.

Henry. My lord of Guise, we understand that you
Have gathered a power of men.
What your intent is yet we cannot learn,
But we presume it is not for our good.   20
Guise. Why, I am no traitor to the crown of France.
What I have done, 'tis for the Gospel's sake.

12.3. SD. *and* Attendants] *Broughton (subst); not in O.*   13. SD. *Gives him money*] *Oliver (subst); not in O.*   13.1. SD. Soldier.] *Broughton (subst);* Soul. *O.*   16.1. SD. *The* Attendants] *Broughton (subst); not in O.*   17. SH. *Henry.*] *Dyce (subst);* King. *O.*   17–20. you / Have ... men. / What ... learn, / But] *Broughton (subst);* you haue ... men, what ... learn, but *O.*   22. Gospel's] *Broughton (subst);* Gospell *O.*

---

8. *free land*] land owned outright.
too free] i.e. sexually promiscuous.
10. *would*] wish.
11. *gear*] i.e. the soldier's musket; penis.
hold] functions properly.
13. *tall*] brave.
15. *list*] wish.
21–2.] Guise may be speaking these lines ironically, in mockery of Navarre's habitual claims that he is fighting not out of dynastic ambition but 'Against the proud disturbers of the faith' (16.3) and 'In honour of our God and country's good' (16.11). Guise's claim to have raised his army 'for the Gospel's sake' seems out of keeping with his extreme Catholicism.

[SC. 19]   THE MASSACRE AT PARIS   109

Épernon. Nay, for the Pope's sake and thine own benefit.
  What peer in France but thou, aspiring Guise,
  Durst be in arms without the King's consent?   25
  I challenge thee for treason in the cause.
Guise. Ah, base Épernon, were not His Highness here,
  Thou shouldst perceive the Duke of Guise is moved.
Henry. Be patient, Guise, and threat not Épernon,
  Lest thou perceive the King of France be moved.   30
Guise. Why? I am a prince of the Valois's line,
  Therefore an enemy to the Bourbonites.
  I am a juror in the Holy League
  And therefore hated of the Protestants.
  What should I do but stand upon my guard?   35
  And, being able, I'll keep a host in pay.
Épernon. Thou able to maintain a host in pay,
  That livest by foreign exhibition!
  The Pope and King of Spain are thy good friends,
  Else all France knows how poor a duke thou art.   40

---

23. SH. *Épernon.*] *Ribner (subst); Eper. O.*   24. thou, aspiring Guise,] *Broughton (subst);* thou (aspiring Guise) *O.*   28. Duke] *Broughton (subst);* D. *O.*   29. SH. *Henry.*] *Dyce (subst); King. O.*   36. a] *O (an).*   37. a] *O (an).*

---

26. *cause*] 'fact, condition of matters, or consideration, moving a person to action; ground of action; reason for action, motive' (*OED*, n., 3a).

28. *moved*] aroused, agitated, angered.

31–2. *I ... Bourbonites*] Guise is referring to the dynastic conflict between the French royal houses of Bourbon and Valois, repeating his earlier claim to be 'kindred to the King' (2.48). Nonetheless, even though the Guises belonged to the royal house of Lorraine and Guise's cousin, Mary Stuart, was married to Henry's older brother Francis II (r. 1559–60) and was therefore briefly Queen of France, Guise's lineage was also extensively intertwined with the house of Bourbon. Guise was the grandson of Claude de Lorraine, Duke of Guise, and Antoinette de Bourbon, and was therefore also kindred to Navarre (Carroll, 311). See note to line 52.

33. *juror*] 'One who takes or has taken an oath; one who swears allegiance to some body or cause' (*OED*, n., 4a).

Holy League] The Catholic League, whose goals were to oppose Navarre and eradicate Protestantism from France. See Holt, 123–4, and Introduction, p. 9.

38. *exhibition*] support, funding, maintenance (*OED*, n., 1a, 2a). As part of his commitment to the Catholic League, Philip of Spain paid Guise a monthly subsidy of 50,000 escudos (Holt, 124).

40. *Else*] otherwise.

Henry. Ay, those are they that feed him with their gold
To countermand our will and check our friends.
Guise. My lord, to speak more plainly, thus it is:
Being animated by religious zeal,
I mean to muster all the power I can 45
To overthrow those sectious Puritans;
And know, my lord, the Pope will sell his triple crown,
Ay, and the Catholic Philip King of Spain,
Ere I shall want, will cause his Indians
To rip the golden bowels of America. 50
Navarre, that cloaks them underneath his wings,
Shall feel the house of Lorraine is his foe.
Your Highness needs not fear mine army's force:
'Tis for your safety and your enemies' wrack.
Henry. Guise, wear our crown, and be thou King of France 55
And as dictator make or war or peace,
Whilst I cry *placet* like a senator.

---

41. SH. *Henry.*] *Dyce (subst); King. O.*   41. Ay] *Broughton (subst);* I *O.*
46. sectious] *Dyce (subst);* sexious *O.*   48. Ay] *Broughton (subst);* I *O.*
55. SH. *Henry.*] *Dyce (subst); King. O.*

---

42. *countermand*] overrule. See *Edward II*, 'proud rebels that are up in arms, / And do confront and countermand their king' (II.187–8).
   check] 'arrest, stop, or retard the onward motion or course of' (*OED*, v.1, 3).
44. *animated*] motivated.
46. *sectious*] sectarian, schismatical. 'Sectious' is Dyce's emendation of O's 'sexious', which the *OED*, citing this usage as its example, declares to be a nonce-word and speculates to mean 'sectarian' (*OED*, sexious, adj.).
47. *triple crown*] papal tiara, which had three tiers.
51. *them*] i.e the 'sectious Puritans' or French Huguenots.
52. *house of Lorraine*] the Dukes of Guise belonged to the royal house of Lorraine, whose founder, René I (1409–80), was Duke of Anjou, Count of Provence, Duke of Bar, Duke of Lorraine, and King of Naples, Aragon, and Jerusalem (Carroll, 310). René belonged to the royal house of Valois-Anjou. See note to lines 31–2.
54. *wrack*] ruin.
55–7.] 'Here, Mortimer, sit thou in Edward's throne; / Warwick and Lancaster, wear you my crown' (4.35–6), Edward protests to his rebellious barons in *Edward II* (Esche, 380).
57. *cry* placet] cry 'it pleases me' (Latin), applaud.
   senator] In times of military crisis, the senate of the Roman Republic would appoint a dictator for a limited term and with clearly specified powers in order to meet the emergency.

SC. 19] THE MASSACRE AT PARIS 111

> I cannot brook thy haughty insolence.
> Dismiss thy camp or else by our edict
> Be thou proclaimed a traitor throughout France.   60

Guise. [*Aside*] The choice is hard. I must dissemble.
> [*To* HENRY] My lord, in token of my true humility
> And simple meaning to Your Majesty,
> I kiss Your Grace's hand and take my leave,
> Intending to dislodge my camp with speed.   65

Henry. Then farewell, Guise. The King and thou are friends.
> *Exit* GUISE.

Épernon. But trust him not, my lord, for had Your Highness
> Seen with what a pomp he entered Paris
> And how the citizens with gifts and shows
> Did entertain him and promised to be at his command—   70
> Nay, they feared not to speak in the streets
> That the Guise durst stand in arms against the King
> For not effecting of His Holiness' will.

Henry. Did they of Paris entertain him so?
> Then means he present treason to our state.   75
> Well, let me alone. Who's within there?

> > > > > *Enter one with a pen and ink.*

> Make a discharge of all my council straight,
> And I'll subscribe my name and seal it straight.
> My head shall be my council—they are false—
> And, Épernon, I will be ruled by thee.   80

---

66. SH. *Henry.*] *Dyce (subst); King. O.*   67. SH. *Épernon.*] *Ribner (subst); Eper. O.*   74. SH. *Henry.*] *Dyce (subst); King. O.*   76. Who's] *Broughton (subst); whose O.*

58.] The line echoes Edward's 'I cannot brook these haughty menaces' (*Edward II*, 1.132).
  brook] bear, tolerate, endure.
  63. *simple*] sincere.
  meaning] motive, intention, purpose (*OED*, n.2, 3).
  65. *dislodge*] Oliver notes that this was 'the regular term for moving a military force' (143).
  73. *effecting*] putting into effect, enacting, implementing.
  His Holiness' will] the canons of the Council of Trent, whose implementation Henry had resisted as a threat to French sovereignty (Holt, 124).
  75. *present*] immediate, impending.
  77.] i.e. write a document that discharges all my council of their duties.
  78. *subscribe*] sign.

Épernon. My lord, I think for safety of your royal person
    It would be good the Guise were made away,
    And so to quit Your Grace of all suspect.
Henry. First let us set our hand and seal to this,
    And then I'll tell thee what I mean to do.   85

            He writes.

    So, convey this to the council presently,

                                    Exit one.

    And, Épernon, though I seem mild and calm,
    Think not but I am tragical within.
    I'll secretly convey me unto Blois,
    For, now that Paris takes the Guise's part,   90
    Here is no staying for the King of France
    Unless he mean to be betrayed and die.
    But as I live, so sure the Guise shall die.

                                    Exeunt.

[SCENE 20]

Enter the King of NAVARRE *reading of a letter, and* BARTAS.

Navarre. My lord, I am advertised from France
    That the Guise hath taken arms against the King

---

81. SH. *Épernon.*] Ribner (subst); Eper. O.   83. quit] Broughton (subst); quite O.   84. SH. *Henry.*] Dyce (subst); King. O.   85.1. SD.] *printed on 85, aligned right, in O.*

Heading Sc. 20] Bullen (subst); not in O.

81–2.] 'Marlowe seems to be the first to make Epernoun responsible for the actual planning of the murder of Guise' (Oliver, 144).
    83.] i.e. and in such a manner as to acquit you from suspicion.
    88. *tragical*] 'Perhaps, as *O.E.D.* has it, "excited with tragic feeling" (2b); perhaps (Bennett) determined on action, against the Guise, that like a tragedy will end in death; perhaps both. See *1H6*, III.i.125, "Why look you still so stern and tragical?"' (Oliver, 144).
    89. *Blois*] city on the Loire River, 180 km south-west of Paris, where Henry convoked a general parliament in October 1588.

[After his victory at Coutras, Navarre continued to campaign against royalist forces until returning to La Rochelle in March 1588. When he learned of Guise's revolt later that year, he offered the King military support. Historically, the King rejected Navarre's offer (Pitts, 131–3).]
    1. *advertised*] warned (*OED*, advertise, v., 1d).

And that Paris is revolted from His Grace.
Bartas. Then hath Your Grace fit opportunity
    To show your love unto the King of France, 5
    Offering him aid against his enemies,
    Which cannot but be thankfully received.
Navarre. Bartas, it shall be so. Post, then, to France,
    And there salute His Highness in our name;
    Assure him all the aid we can provide 10
    Against the Guisians and their complices.
    Bartas, be gone. Commend me to His Grace,
    And tell him ere it be long I'll visit him.
Bartas. I will, my lord.   *Exit.*

                      Enter PLESSIS.

Navarre. Plessis.
Plessis.   My lord. 15
Navarre. Plessis, go muster up our men with speed,
    And let them march away to France amain,
    For we must aid the King against the Guise.
    Be gone, I say. 'Tis time that we were there.
Plessis. I go, my lord. 20
Navarre. That wicked Guise, I fear me much, will be
    The ruin of that famous realm of France,
    For his aspiring thoughts aim at the crown,
    And takes his vantage on religion

---

4. SH. *Bartas.*] *Ribner (subst); Bar. O.*   14. SH. *Bartas.*] *Ribner (subst); Bar. O.*   16. SH. *Navarre.*] *Ribner (subst); Na O.*   21. SH. *Navarre.*] *Ribner (subst); Nauar. O.*

---

   8. *Post*] ride, travel by a relay of horses (*OED*, v.2).
  11. *complices*] accomplices.
  13. *ere*] before.
  17. *amain*] 'with full force, in full force of numbers, at full speed, at once' (*OED*, adv., 1, 2).
  20. *I go*] Some editors, such as Bennett and Esche, have Plessis exit at this point. Following O and Oliver, however, I have kept him on stage until the end of the scene. Oliver comments that 'Editors send Pleshé off the stage here, but O does not (and ends the scene with "*Exeunt*", not "*Exit*"). Pleshé remains to listen to his master's final thoughts; there may even be the implication that Navarre likes an audience for his "sentiments"' (145).
  21–2.] In *Edward II*, Kent declares, 'This Edward is the ruin of the realm' (18.54).
  24. *takes*] he takes.
    vantage on religion] advantage of religion (*OED*, n., 5b).

To plant the Pope and popelings in the realm 25
And bind it wholly to the see of Rome.
But if that God do prosper mine attempts
And send us safely to arrive in France,
We'll beat him back and drive him to his death
That basely seeks the ruin of his realm. 30

Exeunt.

[SCENE 21]

Enter the Captain of the Guard, *and three* Murderers.

Captain. Come on, sirs! What, are you resolutely bent,
Hating the life and honour of the Guise?
What, will you not fear when you see him come?

Heading Sc. 21] *Bullen (subst); not in O.*

25. *popelings*] 'adherents, followers, or subordinates of the Pope; Roman Catholics' (*OED*, n., 1).
26. *see*] bishopric.
27. *if that*] if.

[Guise was assassinated on 23 December 1588. After the Day of Barricades Guise and Henry attempted a reconciliation, and Guise played a prominent role in the general parliament at Blois that began in October. On the morning of the 23rd he was summoned to attend a privy council meeting with the King; from the council room he was called into the King's adjoining private chambers, where he was murdered by the King's royal guards (Carroll, 290–1). Solnon states that Henry had formulated his plan to assassinate Guise by 18 December (Solnon, 358), and modern historians echo Jean Boucher's contention in *La vie et faits notables de Henri de Valois* (1589) that Henry's 'conspiracy was not so secret that Monsieur de Guise did not have some warning of it' (qtd Thomas and Tydeman, 278). Although Guise's defiance of the third Murderer's warning in this scene seems to be Marlowe's own touch, Colynet in *The True History of the Civil Wars of France* (1591) relates that 'the 22 of December, as the Duke of Guise had sat down to dinner, he found under his napkin a little bill wherein was written that he should take heed, for they will play a shrewd play with him. In the same bill he wrote with his own hand a mocking answer thus, "They dare not", and so cast it under the table' (Colynet, 305). As Kocher documents, Marlowe could have culled all the other major details of this scene from various contemporary pamphlet accounts of the assassination on both sides of the confessional divide ('Contemporary Pamphlet Backgrounds', 152–7).]

1. *bent*] set, disposed, determined.

SC. 21]   THE MASSACRE AT PARIS   115

1 Murderer. 'Fear him', said you? Tush, were he here we would
    kill him presently.   5
2 Murderer. Oh, that his heart were leaping in my hand!
3 Murderer. But when will he come, that we may murder
    him?
Captain. Well, then, I see you are resolute.
1 Murderer. Let us alone, I warrant you.
Captain. Then, sirs, take your standings within this
    chamber,   10
    For anon the Guise will come.
All. You will give us our money?
Captain. Ay, ay, fear not. Stand close. So, be resolute.
    Now falls the star whose influence governs France,
    Whose light was deadly to the Protestants.   15
    Now must he fall and perish in his height.

           Enter the King [HENRY] *and* ÉPERNON.

Henry. Now, captain of my guard, are these murderers
    ready?

4. SH. *1 Murderer.*] *Ribner (subst);* 1. *O.*   6. SH. *2 Murderer.*] *Ribner
(subst);* 2. *O.*   7. SH. *3 Murderer.*] *Ribner (subst);* 3. *O.*   8. SH. *Captain.*]
Broughton (subst); Cap. O.   9. SH. *1 Murderer.*] *Ribner (subst);* 1. *O.*   10.
SH. *Captain.*] *Broughton (subst); Cap. O.*   12. money?] *Broughton (subst);*
money. *O.*   13. SH. *Captain.*] *Broughton (subst); Cap. O.*   13. Ay, ay]
Broughton (subst); I, I O.   17. SH. *Henry.*] *Dyce (subst); King. O.*

   6. *heart ... hand*] proverbial (Dent H331, 2).
   9. *I warrant you*] i.e. 'you can rely on us' (Oliver, 146).
   10. *standings*] positions; 'a hunter's station or stand from which to shoot
game' (*OED*, n., 4c).
   this chamber] The Captain might be indicating the discovery space which
in scene 9 was used as Ramus's study and in this scene represents Henry's
royal cabinet. Alternatively, given that the third Murderer later informs
Guise that 'The rest have ta'en their standings in the next room' (61–2), the
Murderers might perhaps conceal themselves behind the tiring house façade
door through which Guise does *not* enter later in the scene.
   11. *anon*] immediately.
   13. *close*] hidden, concealed. The Captain's command, 'Stand close',
might be followed by the Murderers immediately hiding themselves. Henry's
reference to 'these murderers' in line 17, however, suggests that they might
remain on stage to be at least demonstratively gestured at if not directly
addressed by Henry. This editor has chosen the latter option, with the
Captain and the Murderers exiting at the same time after line 21.

116   THE MASSACRE AT PARIS   [SC. 21

Captain. They be, my good lord.
Henry. But are they resolute and armed to kill,
   Hating the life and honour of the Guise?   20
Captain. I warrant ye, my lord.
                         [*Exeunt* Captain *and* Murderers.]
Henry. [*Aside*] Then come, proud Guise, and here disgorge
      thy breast
   Surcharged with surfeit of ambitious thoughts!
   Breathe out that life wherein my death was hid,
   And end thy endless treasons with thy death!   25
         [HENRY *and* ÉPERNON *withdraw into* HENRY'S
                                            royal cabinet.]

              Enter the GUISE *and knocketh.*

Guise. Holà, varlet, hé! Épernon, where is the King?

   [ÉPERNON *enters the main stage from the royal cabinet.*]

Épernon. Mounted his royal cabinet.
Guise. I prithee tell him that the Guise is here.

18. SH. *Captain.*] Broughton *(subst); Cap. O.*   19. SH. *Henry.*] Dyce *(subst); King. O.*   21. SH. *Captain.*] Broughton *(subst); Cap. O.*   21.1. SD.] *this edn; not in O.*   22. SH. *Henry.*] Dyce *(subst); King. O.*   25.1. SD.] *this edn; not in O.*   26. *Holà, varlet, hé*] Dyce *(subst); Halla verlete hey O.*   26.1. SD.] *this edn; not in O.*   27. SH. *Épernon.*] Ribner *(subst); Eper. O.*

21.1. SD.] The Murderers might exit by actually exiting or by concealing themselves at various points on the stage.
   22. *disgorge*] discharge or empty (*OED*, v., 2a, citing this instance).
   23. *Surcharged*] overcharged, overloaded, overburdened (*OED*, adj., a).
   surfeit] excess.
   25.1. SD. royal cabinet] i.e. Henry's private chambers, which may on stage be represented by the discovery space behind the tiring house façade's main doors. See Introduction, pp. 40–1.
   25.2. SD.] Guise might enter through one of the side stage doors and 'knock' on the discovery space, which he then enters at line 32.
   26. Holà, varlet, hé!] 'Hello there, page' (Spanish); see Oliver, 147.
   27. *Mounted*] ascended, entered into.
   cabinet] private chamber (*OED*, n., 3), bedroom.

SC. 21]   THE MASSACRE AT PARIS   117

Épernon. An't please Your Grace, the Duke of Guise doth crave
    Access unto Your Highness.

                [HENRY *enters*]

Henry.   Let him come in.   30
    [*Aside*] Come, Guise, and see thy traitorous guile outreached,
    And perish in the pit thou mad'st for me.

        The GUISE *comes to the King* [HENRY].

Guise. Good morrow to Your Majesty.
Henry. Good morrow to my loving cousin of Guise.
    How fares it this morning with Your Excellence?   35
Guise. I heard Your Majesty was scarcely pleased
    That in the court I bare so great a train.
Henry. They were to blame that said I was displeased,
    And you, good cousin, to imagine it.
    'Twere hard with me if I should doubt my kin   40
    Or be suspicious of my dearest friends.
    Cousin, assure you I am resolute,
    Whatsoever any whisper in mine ears,
    Not to suspect disloyalty in thee.
    And so, sweet coz, farewell.   45
                Exit King [HENRY, *and* ÉPERNON.]
Guise. So, now sues the King for favour to the Guise,
    And all his minions stoop when I command.
    Why, this 'tis to have an army in the field.

---

29. SH. *Épernon.*] *Ribner (subst); Eper. O.* 29. An't] *Broughton (subst); And O.* 29-30. crave / Access] *Broughton (subst);* crave access *O.* 30. SD.] *this edn; not in O.* 30. SH. *Henry.*] *Dyce (subst);* King. *O.* 32.1. SD.] *aligned right O.* 34. SH. *Henry.*] *Dyce (subst);* King. *O.* 38. SH. *Henry.*] *Dyce (subst);* King. *O.*

---

   29. *An't*] if it.
   32. *pit*] trap.
   37. *train*] retinue.
   40. *'Twere ... me*] i.e. I would be obstinate, unfeeling, or stupid.
   49. *holy sacrament*] Eucharist, the communion wafer celebrated as the body of Christ during Mass.

> Now by the holy sacrament I swear:
> As ancient Romans over their captive lords, 50
> So will I triumph over this wanton King,
> And he shall follow my proud chariot's wheels.
> Now do I but begin to look about,
> And all my former time was spent in vain.
> Hold, sword, for in thee is the Duke of Guise's hope. 55

Enter one of the Murderers.

> Villain, why dost thou look so ghastly? Speak.
> *3 Murderer.* Oh, pardon me, my lord of Guise.
> *Guise.* Pardon thee? Why, what hast thou done?
> *3 Murderer.* O my lord, I am one of them that is set to murder
> you. 60
> *Guise.* To murder me, villain?
> *3 Murderer.* Ay, my lord. The rest have ta'en their standings
> in the next room; therefore, good my lord, go not forth.
> *Guise.* Yet Caesar shall go forth!

---

57. SH. *3 Murderer.*] *Ribner (subst); Mur. O.*   59. SH. *3 Murderer.*] *Ribner (subst); Mur. O.*   62. SH. *3 Murderer.*] *Ribner (subst); Mur. O.*   62. Ay] *Broughton (subst);* I *O.*   64-7. forth. / Let ... death. / Tut ... Guise, / And] *Broughton (subst);* forth, let ... death: tut ... Guise: and *O.*

51-2. *triumph ... wheels*] To celebrate their military triumphs, victorious Roman generals paraded through the streets of Rome, their chariots preceded by captives and spoils of war. Guise imagines Henry following his chariot. The lines echo *2 Henry VI*, 2.4.13-14: 'That erst did follow thy proud chariot-wheels / When thou didst ride in triumph through the streets.'

51. *wanton*] undisciplined, ungoverned, unruly, naughty (*OED*, adj., 1a).

53. *look about*] i.e. see my situation clearly.

54.] Guise may be suggesting that he now sees that direct military action is (or at this moment appears to be) far more effective than the strategy of intrigue that he formerly pursued.

55.1. SD.] The Murderer might 'enter' simply by stepping out of hiding. Alternatively, he might enter from the side stage door.

56. *ghastly*] See *Julius Caesar* 1.3.23-4.

64.] Shakespeare echoes this line exactly in *Julius Caesar*, 2.2.28. Guise compares himself to Caesar earlier in the play, at 2.95, and repeats the comparison at line 82 of this scene. In *An Excellent Discourse upon the now present estate of France* (1592), Michel Hurault compares Guise's assassination to 'the murder of the dictator Caesar', which 'served for a pretence to Antony and Augustus to overthrow the Roman commonwealth' (Hurault, fol. 2^v).

SC. 21] THE MASSACRE AT PARIS 119

    Let mean conceits and baser men fear death. 65
    Tut, they are peasants; I am Duke of Guise,
    And princes with their looks engender fear.

        [*1 Murderer and 2 Murderer enter.*]

1 Murderer. [*Aside to 2 Murderer*] Stand close, he is coming.
    I know him by his voice.
Guise. As pale as ashes. Nay, then, 'tis time to look about.
All. Down with him! Down with him! 70

        They stab him.

Guise. Oh, I have my death's wound. Give me leave to
    speak.
2 Murderer. Then pray to God, and ask forgiveness of the
    King.
Guise. Trouble me not. I ne'er offended Him,
    Nor will I ask forgiveness of the King.
    Oh, that I have not power to stay my life, 75
    Nor immortality to be revenged!
    To die by peasants, what a grief is this?
    Ah, Sixtus, be revenged upon the King;

67.1. SD. *1 Murderer and 2 Murderer enter.*] this edn; not in O.   68. SH. *1 Murderer.*] Ribner (subst); *1. O.*   70.1. SD.] aligned right O.   72. SH. *2 Murderer.*] Ribner (subst); *2. O.*   78. Sixtus] Dyce 2 (subst); Sextus O. 82. messe] Broughton (subst); messa O.

---

    65. *mean conceits*] common, base, or ignoble thoughts.
    67.1. SD.] O gives these two Murderers no entrance stage direction before they materialise to murder Guise at line 69. Presumably, they 'enter' the scene in the same manner as the third Murderer, from the 'next room' (61), the rather indeterminate location in which they and the other Murderer have been hiding for the duration of Guise's conversation with Henry.
    69. *As ... ashes*] After comparing himself to Caesar at 2.95, Guise declares that 'Those that hate me will I learn to loathe' (96) and asks for 'a look that, when I bend the brows, / Pale death may walk in furrows of my face' (97–8). Bennett suggests that Guise is referring 'to the ghastly look of the murderer' (239).
    73. *Him*] God.
    75. *stay*] keep, retain, prolong.
    78. *Sixtus*] Pope Sixtus V (1585–90).

Philip and Parma, I am slain for you.
Pope, excommunicate, Philip, depose 80
The wicked branch of cursed Valois his line.
Vive la messe! Perish Huguenots!
Thus Caesar did go forth, and thus he died.

He dies.

Enter Captain of the Guard.

Captain. What, have you done? Then stay awhile,
And I'll go call the King. But see where he comes. 85

[*Enter* HENRY *and* ÉPERNON *with attendants.*]

My lord, see where the Guise is slain.
Henry. Ah, this sweet sight is physic to my soul.
Go fetch his son for to behold his death.

[*Exit an attendant.*]

Surcharged with guilt of thousand massacres,
Monsieur of Lorraine, sink away to hell! 90
And in remembrance of those bloody broils
To which thou didst allure me, being alive,
And here in presence of you all, I swear

83.1. SD.] *printed on 82, aligned right, in O.* 84–5. awhile, / And] *this edn;* a while, and *O.* 85.1. SD.] Broughton (subst); *not in O.* 87. SH. *Henry.*] Dyce (subst); *King. O.* 88.1. SD.] Dyce (subst); *not in O.*

79. *Philip*] Philip II of Spain (r. 1556–98).
Parma] Alessandro Farnese, Duke of Parma (1545–92), the Spanish general who led Spanish forces against Protestant Netherlands and England.
80. *excommunicate*] formally expel from the Church. Queen Elizabeth was excommunicated by the Pope in 1570 (Guy, 277). By excommunicating a monarch, the Pope freed that monarch's Catholic subjects from their allegiance to her or him and thus opened the door to her or his assassination or deposition. The Pope excommunicated Henry III in May 1589 (Pitts, 141).
81. *Valois his*] Valois's.
82. Vive la messe!] 'Long live the Mass!' (French).
87. *physic*] medicine; 'mental, moral, or spiritual remedy' (*OED*, n., 2b).
88. *for to*] in order to.
90. *Monsieur of Lorraine*] Guise. Noting that 'as the title Monsieur was given to princely members of a royal house, it is inappropriate unless the King is using it with irony', Esche states that '[t]he context of strong invective raises the possibility that the word should be "Monster"' (399).

I ne'er was King of France until this hour.
This is the traitor that hath spent my gold 95
In making foreign wars and civil broils.
Did he not draw a sort of English priests
From Douai to the seminary at Reims
To hatch forth treason 'gainst their natural queen?
Did he not cause the King of Spain's huge fleet 100
To threaten England and to menace me?
Did he not injure Monsieur that's deceased?
Hath he not made me in the Pope's defence
To spend the treasure that should strength my land
In civil broils between Navarre and me? 105

---

102. deceased] *OBL, OBod, OCh, OFo, OLC, OMa, OPa, OVAM (subst);* diceast *OHu, ONe.*

94.] Hurault recounts that Henry 'did no sooner see his enemy dead but by and by he believed he had no more enemies in the world, and indeed it is most certain that among his familiars he gave out these speeches: "This day I am king"' – and then adds 'and yet contrawise even the same day he began not to be so' (Hurault, fol. 2ᵛ). Oliver notes that 'This comment, recorded by many of the historians, became famous' (151).

97. *sort*] kind.

98. *Douai ... Reims*] In 1578 the Cardinal of Guise aided the relocation of the English Jesuit seminary, where English Catholic exiles were trained to return to England as missionaries and political agitators, from Douai to Reims (Carroll, 242).

99.] English Jesuit priests who trained in European Catholic seminaries such as Douai and Reims and then returned to England as missionaries and priests to the English Catholic community were routinely suspected of and charged with treason, especially after Queen Elizabeth was excommunicated in 1570. Edmund Campion, executed in 1581, is the best-known example. Along with his absent English Jesuit superiors, Campion was accused of 'having conspired together in Rome and Rheims to imagine, contrive and compass not merely the deposition of the Queen but her death and final destruction' (Plowden, 324).

100. *King ... fleet*] the Spanish Armada, which sailed against England, and was defeated, in 1588.

102.] Contemporary pamphlets alleged that Guise attempted to have Henry's younger brother Alençon assassinated (Kocher, 'Contemporary Pamphlet Backgrounds Part Two', 311). Before he died in 1584, Alençon was one of Queen Elizabeth's marriage suitors (Plowden, 505).

105. *civil broils*] i.e. the French Wars of Religion, which plunged France into civil war between 1562 and 1593.

Tush, to be short, he meant to make me monk
Or else to murder me, and so be king.
Let Christian princes that shall hear of this
(As all the world shall know our Guise is dead)
Rest satisfied with this that here I swear: 110
Ne'er was there king of France so yoked as I.
Épernon. My lord, here is his son.

Enter [an attendant with] the GUISE'S *son* [YOUNG GUISE].

Henry. Boy, look where your father lies.
Young Guise. My father slain? Who hath done this deed?
Henry. Sirrah, 'twas I that slew him and will slay   115
Thee too, an thou prove such a traitor.
Young Guise. Art thou King and hast done this bloody deed?
I'll be revenged!

He offereth to throw his dagger.

Henry. Away to prison with him. I'll clip his wings
Or ere he pass my hands. Away with him.   120
Exit [an attendant with the] boy [YOUNG GUISE].

---

112. SH. *Épernon.*] Ribner *(subst); Eper. O.* 112.1. SD. *an attendant with*] *this edn; not in O.* 113. SH. *Henry.*] Dyce *(subst); King. O.* 115. SH. *Henry.*] Dyce *(subst); King. O.* 115–16. slay / Thee] Broughton *(subst);* slay thee *O.* 116. an] Broughton *(subst);* and *O.* 119. SH. *Henry.*] Dyce *(subst); King. O.* 119–20. wings / Or] Broughton *(subst);* winges or *O.* 120.1. SD. *an attendant with the*] Broughton *(subst); not in O.*

106–7.] Colynet claimed that Guise intended to 'take the King and his mother, either put them in monkeries, or else to rid them out of this world' (8).

111. *yoked*] bound, restricted, constrained.

114. SH. Young Guise] Charles de Lorraine (1571–1640), Prince of Joinville.

116. *an*] if.

117–18.] *Les Cruatés Sanguinaires* relates that Guise's son, 'ne pouvant baiser son père pour lui dire le dernier adieu, commence à vomir un infinité de paroles injurieuses contre les massacreurs de son père' ['unable to embrace his father and say his last goodbye, began to vomit an infinity of injurious speeches against the murderers of his father'] (qtd Kocher, 'Contemporary Pamphlet Backgrounds', 156).

118.1. SD. offereth] attempts.

119. *Away ... him*] Charles was imprisoned for three years at Tours.

120. *Or ... hands*] i.e. before he passes out of my hands.

But what availeth that this traitor's dead
When Duke Dumaine, his brother, is alive
And that young Cardinal that is grown so proud?
[*To the* Captain of the Guard] Go to the Governor of
 Orléans
And will him in my name to kill the Duke.   125
                    [*Exit* Captain of the Guard.]
[*To the* Murderers] Get you away and strangle the
 Cardinal.
                          [*Exeunt* Murderers.]
These two will make one entire Duke of Guise,
Especially with our old mother's help.
Épernon. My lord, see where she comes, as if she drooped
 To hear these news.   130

    Enter QUEEN MOTHER [CATHERINE, with attendants].

Henry. And let her droop. My heart is light enough.
 Mother, how like you this device of mine?
 I slew the Guise because I would be King.
Catherine. King? Why, so thou wert before.
 Pray God thou be a king now this is done.   135

125.1. SD.] *Broughton (subst); not in O.*   126.1. SD.] *Broughton (subst); not in O.*   129. SH. Épernon.] *Ribner (subst); Eper. O.*   129–30. drooped / To] *Dyce (subst);* droupt to *O.*   131. SH. *Henry.*] *Dyce (subst); King. O.*   134. SH. *Catherine.*] *Ribner (subst); Queene. O.*

---

121. *what availeth*] i.e. what use or benefit is it.
125. *will*] order, command.
127.] i.e. the two brothers combined will make as much trouble as Guise did by himself.
130. *these news*] i.e. the news of Guise's murder.
132–5.] Serres in *A General Inventorie of the History of France* (1598) writes that 'The execution done, the King carries news thereof to the Queen Mother. "Madame", saith he, "I will hereafter reign alone, I have no more companions". She answered him, "God grant, my son, it fall out well for you"' (725).
132. *this ... mine*] Henry might here gesture towards Guise's body, which remains on stage until the end of the scene. The use of 'device' might be intended to embrace two contemporary meanings: 'Something devised ... for bringing about some end or result' (*OED*, n.6) and an 'emblematic figure' (*OED*, n.9) representing Henry's success in removing the obstacle to his own ambitions.

Henry. Nay, he was King and countermanded me,
   But now I will be King and rule myself
   And make the Guisians stoop that are alive.
Catherine. I cannot speak for grief. When thou wast born,
   I would that I had murdered thee, my son.   140
   My son? Thou art a changeling, not my son.
   I curse thee and exclaim thee miscreant,
   Traitor to God and to the realm of France.
Henry. Cry out, exclaim, howl till thy throat be hoarse!
   The Guise is slain, and I rejoice therefore.   145
   And now will I to arms. Come, Épernon,
   And let her grieve her heart out if she will.
                  Exit the King [HENRY] *and* ÉPERNON.
Catherine. Away, leave me alone to meditate.
   Sweet Guise, would he had died so thou wert here.
   To whom shall I bewray my secrets now,   150
   Or who will help to build religion?
   The Protestants will glory and insult,
   Wicked Navarre will get the crown of France,
   The Popedom cannot stand, all goes to wrack,
   And all for thee, my Guise! What may I do?   155

---

136. SH. *Henry.*] Dyce *(subst)*; King. *O.* 139. SH. *Catherine.*] Ribner *(subst)*; Queene. *O.* 141. son?] Bullen *(subst)*; sonne: *O.* 144. SH. *Henry.*] Dyce *(subst)*; King. *O.* 148. SH. *Catherine.*] Ribner *(subst)*; Queene. *O.*

---

136. *countermanded*] overruled; see note to 19.42.
138. *stoop*] bow to superior power or authority; humble oneself, yield obedience (*OED*, v.1., 2a).
140. *would*] wish.
141. *changeling*] a baby surreptitiously substituted for a mother's real child at birth. See the Duchess of York's denunciation of her son, Richard III: 'Thou cam'st on earth to make earth my hell. / A grievous burden was thy birth to me' (*Richard III*, 4.4.167–8)
142. *exclaim*] express by exclamation (*OED*, v., 3, citing this as first instance).
   miscreant] misbeliever, heretic.
150. *bewray*] reveal, divulge, disclose (*OED*, v., 4).
154. *wrack*] ruin.

SC. 22]   THE MASSACRE AT PARIS   125

   But sorrow seize upon my toiling soul,
   For since the Guise is dead, I will not live.
   [*Exeunt* CATHERINE *and attendants, with* GUISE's *body*].

                        [SCENE 22]

         Enter two [Murderers] *dragging in the* CARDINAL.

Cardinal. Murder me not! I am a cardinal!
1 Murderer. Wert thou the Pope thou mightst not scape
   from us.
Cardinal. What, will you file your hands with churchmen's
   blood?
2 Murderer. Shed your blood? O Lord, no, for we intend to
   strangle you.
Cardinal. Then there is no remedy but I must die?   5

157.1. SD.] *this edn; Exit O.*

Heading Sc. 22] *Bullen (subst); not in O.* 1. SH. *Cardinal.*] *Ribner (subst); Car. O.* 2. SH. *1 Murderer.*] *Ribner (subst); 1. O.* 3. SH. *Cardinal.*] *Ribner (subst); Car. O.* 4. SH. *2 Murderer.*] *Ribner (subst); 2. O.* 5. SH. *Cardinal.*] *Ribner (subst); Car. O.* 5. die?] *Bullen (subst); dye. O.*

   157. *I ... live*] Serres relates that 'transported with grief', Catherine 'died the fifth of January following' (*General Inventorie*, 725).
   157.1. SD] Attendants have been added to Catherine's entrance at 129.1 SD in order that here, at the end of the scene, they can take Guise's body with them and thus clear the stage for the next scene. Alternatively, Henry and Épernon could carry the body off the stage when they exit at 147.1 SD, or Catherine could lug the guts by herself. Either alternative would eliminate the need for attendants. The body could also be left on stage for the Murderers to carry off at the end of the next scene along with the corpse of Guise's brother, the Cardinal.
   [The Cardinal was arrested immediately after his brother's assassination (Solnon, 361) and murdered the following day, Christmas Eve, in his prison cell by six soldiers, each of whom was paid 200 livres for his service. His body, like his brother's, was then burnt (Carroll, 292). Contemporary accounts differ on the manner of the Cardinal's death, some claiming that he was strangled and others that his murderers used their swords (Kocher, 'Contemporary Pamphlet Backgrounds', 158). Marlowe chooses strangulation in this scene, as he does in 4.1 of *The Jew of Malta*.]
   3. *file*] defile.

126   THE MASSACRE AT PARIS   [SC. 23

1 Murderer. No remedy. Therefore prepare yourself.
Cardinal. Yet lives my brother, Duke Dumaine, and many
          more
     To revenge our deaths upon that cursed King,
     Upon whose heart may all the Furies grip
     And with their paws drench his black soul in hell.   10
1 Murderer. Yours, my Lord Cardinal, you should have said.

            Now they strangle him.

     So, pluck amain! He is hard-hearted, therefore pull with
     violence. Come, take him away.
                                                  Exeunt.

                    [SCENE 23]

     Enter Duke DUMAINE *reading of a letter, with others.*

Dumaine. My noble brother murdered by the King!
     Oh, what may I do for to revenge thy death?

6. SH. *1 Murderer.*] *Ribner; 1. O.*   7. SH. *Cardinal.*] *Ribner (subst); Car. O.*
more] *O (moe).*   9. grip] *O (gripe).*   11. SH. *1 Murderer.*] *Ribner (subst);*
1. O.

Heading Sc. 23] *Bullen (subst); not in O.*   1. by] *OBL, OBod, OCh, OFo,*
OLC, OMa, OPa, OVAM (subst); dy OHu, ONe.

   9–10.] Bennett compares *2 Tamburlaine* 3.5.24–9, in which Orcanes envisions 'legions of devils' (25) who have 'monstrous paws' (28) and 'guard the gates' (29) of the 'lake of hell' (24), to which Orcanes intends to send Tamburlaine's soul (Bennett, 244).
   9. *Furies*] goddesses of vengeance in classical myth, often represented as bird-like creatures.
   10. *paws*] feet or claws of a bird or dragon (*OED*, n.1, 1a).
   drench] submerge, drown (*OED*, v., 2).
   12. *pluck amain*] i.e. pull as hard as you can. See 4.1 of *Jew of Malta*, in which Barabas and Ithimore strangle Friar Barnardine. Like the Cardinal's two murderers, Barabas and Ithimore joke with their victim before they murder him. As they strangle the friar, Ithimore urges his master to 'pull amain' (148), and after the friar is dead Barabas commands his slave to 'Take him [the friar's body] up' (150).
   hard-hearted] unmerciful; following Craik, Esche also suggests 'difficult to kill' (401).
   [Contemporary sources place the Duke of Mayenne at Lyon rather than Orléans (Kocher, 'Contemporary Pamphlet Backgrounds', 159). Historically, Henry sent the colonel of Ornano to Lyon to assassinate Mayenne, but he was forewarned and fled (Solnon, 362).]

SC. 23]   THE MASSACRE AT PARIS   127

  The King's alone, it cannot satisfy.
  Sweet Duke of Guise, our prop to lean upon,
  Now thou art dead here is no stay for us. 5
  I am thy brother, and I'll revenge thy death,
  And root Valois his line from forth of France,
  And beat proud Bourbon to his native home
  That basely seeks to join with such a king,
  Whose murderous thoughts will be his overthrow. 10
  He willed the Governor of Orléans in his name
  That I with speed should have been put to death,
  But that's prevented, for to end his life—
  His life, and all those traitors to the Church of Rome
  That durst attempt to murder noble Guise. 15

     Enter the Friar.

Friar. My lord, I come to bring you news that your brother
  the Cardinal of Lorraine by the King's consent is lately
  strangled unto death.
Dumaine. My brother Cardinal slain, and I alive?
  Oh, words of power to kill a thousand men! 20
  Come, let us away and levy men:
  'Tis war that must assuage this tyrant's pride.

  4–5.] These lines echo *The True Tragedy*, 'Sweet Duke of York, our prop to lean upon, / Now thou art gone there is no hope for us' (sig. B4ʳ).
  4. *prop*] support.
  5. *stay*] support, prop (*OED*, n.2, 1a).
  7. *Valois his*] Valois's.
  10. *his*] i.e. Henry III's.
  11. *He*] Henry III.
  13. *prevented*] precluded, stopped, hindered (*OED*, v., 9).
  14.] The hypermetricality of this line led its first modern editor, Oxberry, to omit the opening 'His life'. Esche concurs, asserting that O's repetition of 'His life' at the beginning of l.14 is a compositor's eye slip (402). Oliver, however, retains O's repetition, arguing that '[t]he repetition of the two words from the end of the preceding line may well be a compositor's error but may also be another attempt to render the process of thought' (157).
  16. SH. Friar] historically, Jacques Clément, a young Jacobin monk whose curé was Jean Boucher, the vehemently anti-Huguenot author of *Histoire tragique et memorable de Piers Gaveston* (1588) (Solnon, 379).
  20–1.] These lines echo Edward's response to the barons' assault on his favourite, Gaveston, in *Edward the Second*: 'Come, Edmund, let's away and levy men. / 'Tis war that must abate these barons' pride' (6.97–8).

128   THE MASSACRE AT PARIS   [SC. 24

Friar. My lord, hear me but speak. I am a friar
　Of the order of the Jacobins
　That for my conscience' sake will kill the King.   25
Dumaine. But what doth move thee above the rest to do the deed?
Friar. O my lord, I have been a great sinner in my days, and the deed is meritorious.
Dumaine. But how wilt thou get opportunity?   30
Friar. Tush, my lord, let me alone for that.
Dumaine. Friar, come with me. We will go talk more of this within.

　　　　　　　　　　　　　　　　　Exeunt.

[SCENE 24]

Sound drum and trumpets, and enter the King of France [HENRY], *and* NAVARRE, ÉPERNON, BARTAS, PLESSIS *and* Soldiers.

Henry. Brother of Navarre, I sorrow much
　That ever I was proved your enemy
　And that the sweet and princely mind you bear
　Was ever troubled with injurious wars.
　I vow as I am lawful King of France   5

23–4. friar / Of] *this edn;* speak, / I *O.*   32. me. We] *this edn;* me, / We *O;* me; we *Oliver (subst).*

Heading Sc. 24] *Bullen (subst); not in O.*   1. SH. Henry.] *Dyce (subst);* King. *O.*

---

24. *Jacobins*] Dominicans, whose college in Paris was on rue Saint-Jacques (Solnon, 388).
28. *great sinner*] Colynet describes Clément as 'such a one as for his lewdness and for being taken oftentimes in stews and whorehouses had been by the order of the discipline diversely punished' (402).
29. *the ... is meritorious*] *2 Henry VI*, 3.1.270 echoes this phrase exactly. Radical Catholics such as Boucher argued that it was a good deed to kill a tyrant, especially one who had been excommunicated (Henry was excommunicated in May 1589) (Solnon, 387). Kocher observes that Protestant writers accused Catholics of teaching 'that assassination of rulers dangerous to the Church was "meritorious," in the sense that it would earn the assassin a place in Heaven' ('Contemporary Pamphlet Backgrounds', 160).

[1 August 1589, Henry III's château at St-Cloud, just outside Paris.]

  To recompense your reconciled love
  With all the honours and affections
  That ever I vouchsafed my dearest friends.
Navarre. It is enough if that Navarre may be
  Esteemed faithful to the King of France,   10
  Whose service he may still command till death.
Henry. Thanks to my kingly brother of Navarre.
  Then here we'll lie before Lutetia's walls,
  Girting this strumpet city with our siege,
  Till, surfeiting with our afflicting arms,   15
  She cast her hateful stomach to the earth.

       Enter a Messenger.

Messenger. An it please Your Majesty, here is a friar of the order of the Jacobins sent from the President of Paris, that craves access unto Your Grace.

---

12. SH. *Henry.*] *Dyce (subst); King. O.*   13. Lutetia's] *Broughton (subst);* Lucrecia *O.*   17. An] *Broughton (subst);* And *O.*

---

  8. *vouchsafed*] gave, granted, bestowed upon.
  11. *Whose*] Navarre's.
  he] Henry III.
  13. *Lutetia's*] Paris's. Paris was known as 'Lutetia' during the Roman Empire. Ironically, Henry here adopts one of Guise's favourite roles, the role of Julius Caesar, whose forces defeated the rebellious Gauls at the Battle of Lutetia during the Gallic Wars (Caesar, *Gallic War*, 7.57–62).
  lie] encamp.
  14. *Girting*] surrounding (*OED*, v., 1).
  strumpet] whore, prostitute. Paris is 'so called because it had proved faithless to the King, by espousing the cause of Guise' (Oliver, 158). Esche adds that 'for an English audience the phrase might also suggest the "Strumpet of Rome" or the "Babylonian Strumpet"' (402).
  15–16.] 'The image – not perfectly appropriate – is of the city's being given a surfeit or "overdose" of warfare and therefore vomiting its stomach (with a probable quibble on "stomach" in the sense of "pride")' (Oliver, 158).
  15. *surfeiting*] becoming ill through excess (*OED*, v., 3a).
  afflicting arms] assaulting weapons.
  16. *cast*] vomit.
  18. *President of Paris*] the chief official of France's highest judicial body, the Parlement of Paris, by which all royal edicts had to be recorded and approved in order to pass into force (Jouanna, 65). Contemporary pamphlet sources identify him as '"the first President of the Senate named President Harlay," one of the King's party at that time held in prison in Paris' (Kocher, 'Contemporary Pamphlet Backgrounds', 161).

130   THE MASSACRE AT PARIS   [SC. 24

Henry. Let him come in.   20

              Enter Friar *with a letter.*

Épernon. I like not this friar's look.
'Twere not amiss, my lord, if he were searched.
Henry. Sweet Épernon, our friars are holy men
    And will not offer violence to their king
    For all the wealth and treasure of the world.   25
    Friar, thou dost acknowledge me thy King?
Friar. Ay, my good lord, and will die therein.
Henry. Then come thou near and tell what news thou bringst.
Friar. My lord,
    The President of Paris greets Your Grace   30
    And sends his duty by these speedy lines,
    Humbly craving your gracious reply.
Henry. I'll read them, friar, and then I'll answer thee.
Friar. Sancte Iacobe, now have mercy upon me.

---

20. SH. *Henry.*] *Dyce (subst);* King. *O.* 23. SH. *Henry.*] *Dyce (subst);* King. *O.* 26. King?] *Broughton (subst);* King: *O.* 27. Ay] *Broughton (subst);* I *O.* 28. SH. *Henry.*] *Dyce (subst);* King. *O.* 29–32. lord, / The ... Grace / And ... lines, / Humbly] *Broughton (subst);* Lord, the ... grace, and ... lines, humblye *O.* 31. sends] *OBL, OBod, OCh, OFo, OLC, OMa, OPa, OVAM (subst);* send *OHu, ONe.* 33. SH. *Henry.*] *Dyce (subst);* King. *O.* 34. Iacobe] *Dyce (subst);* Iacobus *O.* 34.1–2 SD.] *aligned right O.*

    23–4. *our ... king*] Colynet suggests that, when selecting their assassin, the conspirators behind the plot, 'advising themselves of the King's more than superstitious heart, concluded to make choice of some saucy desperate wretch who, covered with the cloak of hypocrisy, might pierce through all the graces of the King's house without any suspicion of examination' (400). Serres relates that 'The King (who, for the reverence he bare unto Church men, gave free access unto such as under the habit of religion made show to be devoted unto the service of God) commands he [Clément] should be brought into his chamber' (*General Inventorie*, 736).
    31. *speedy*] written in haste.
    34. Sancte Iacobe] 'Saint James' (Latin).
    34.1–2 SD.] Serres narrates the action as follows: 'The King did no sooner begin to read it [the letter], but this wretch, seeing himself alone, grows resolute and, drawing a knife out of his sleeve, made of purpose, thrust His Majesty into the bottom of the belly and there leaves the knife in the wound. The King draws it forth and, with some striving of the monk, strikes him above the eye. Many ran in at this noise and, in the heat of choler killing this monster of men, prevented the true discovery of this enterprise and the authors thereof' (*General Inventorie*, 736).

SC. 24]   THE MASSACRE AT PARIS   131

He stabs the King with a knife as he readeth the letter,
and then the King getteth the knife and kills him.

Épernon. O my lord, let him live awhile.   35
Henry. No, let the villain die and feel in hell
  Just torments for his treachery!
Navarre. What, is Your Highness hurt?
Henry. Yes, Navarre, but not to death, I hope.
Navarre. God shield Your Grace from such a sudden death.   40
  Go call a surgeon hither straight.
Henry. What irreligious pagans' parts be these,
  Of such as hold them of the Holy Church?
  Take hence that damnèd villain from my sight.
Épernon. Ah, had Your Highness let him live,   45
  We might have punished him to his deserts.
Henry. Sweet Épernon, all rebels under heaven
  Shall take example by his punishment
  How they bear arms against their sovereign.
  Go call the English agent hither straight.   50

---

36. SH. *Henry.*] *Dyce (subst); King. O.*   36–7. hell / Just] *Broughton (subst);* hell, iust *O.*   39. SH. *Henry.*] *Dyce (subst); King. O.*   42. SH. *Henry.*] *Dyce (subst); King. O.*   45. SH. *Épernon.*] *Ribner (subst); Eper. O.*   47. SH. *Henry.*] *Dyce (subst); King. O.*   47–9. heaven / Shall ... punishment / How] *Broughton (subst);* heauen, shall ... punishment, how *O.*   48. his] *Broughton (subst);* their *O.*

---

41. *straight*] immediately.
42. *parts*] 'aspects or constituents *of* a quality or action, considered apart from the whole' (*OED*, n.1, 5). The Friar's murderous action is pagan and irreligious even though he is as a whole a Christian Friar of the Catholic Church. Henry is perplexed by the incongruity.
43. *hold them*] i.e. consider themselves to be members.
46. *to his deserts*] i.e. as he deserved.
50.] According to Colynet, 'The King, having made an end of his prayers, sendeth for his brother the King of Navarre, and for the chiefest lords of his court, governors and captains, but specially for the heads of the strangers, to the intent that if it were God's will that he should die they might know his last will' (407).
  agent] ambassador. The English ambassador at this time was Sir Edward Stafford. In response to Henry's summons, however, he sent his *chargé d'affaires*, William Lyly, who wrote a same-day report of the assassination to Queen Elizabeth (Potter, 89). According to Esche, 'Roma Gill suggests (privately) that Marlowe is in fact bringing his patron, Sir Thomas Walsingham (1568–1630), onto the stage, but the "Agent" is more likely to be Sir Francis Walsingham (1530?–90), who was not actually in France at

I'll send my sister England news of this
And give her warning of her treacherous foes.

[*Enter* Surgeon.]

Navarre. Pleaseth Your Grace to let the surgeon search your
   wound.
Henry. The wound, I warrant ye, is deep, my lord.
Search, surgeon, and resolve me what thou seest.   55

The Surgeon *searcheth.*

Enter the English Agent.

Agent for England, send thy mistress word
What this detested Jacobin hath done.
Tell her for all this that I hope to live,
Which if I do, the papal monarch goes to wrack
And antichristian kingdom falls.   60
These bloody hands shall tear his triple crown
And fire accursèd Rome about his ears.
I'll fire his crasèd buildings and incense

52.1. SD.] *Broughton (subst); not in O.*   54. SH. *Henry.*] *Dyce (subst); King. O.*   55. thou seest] *OBL, OBod, OCh, OFo, OLC, OMa, OPa, OVAM (subst);* thou thou seest *OHu, ONe.*

---

this historical moment, but had been there from December 1570 to April 1573 as the English ambassador' (403).
   51. *sister England*] Queen Elizabeth.
   55.2. SD. *English Agent*] William Lyly (see note to line 50).
   56–8.] In his report to Elizabeth, Lyly states that Henry told him that 'I am sure the Queen your mistress will be sorry for this, but I hope it shall quickly be healed, and so I pray write unto her from me' (Potter, 89).
   59–67.] The lines echo Edward's tirade against papal authority in 4.96–103 of Marlowe's *Edward the Second*: 'Why should a king be subject to a priest? / Proud Rome, that hatchest such imperial grooms, / For these thy superstitious taper-lights, / Wherewith thy antichristian churches blaze, / I'll fire thy crazèd buildings and enforce / The papal towers to kiss the lowly ground, / With slaughtered priests make Tiber's channel swell, / And banks raised higher with their sepulchres.'
   59. *papal monarch*] Pope.
   60. *antichristian kingdom*] papacy.
   61. *triple crown*] See note to 19.47.
   62. *fire*] set fire to, ignite.
   63. *crasèd*] cracked, unsound, diseased (*OED*, adj., 1, 3, 4).
   incense] move, cause.

The papal towers to kiss the holy earth.
Navarre, give me thy hand. I here do swear 65
To ruinate that wicked Church of Rome
That hatcheth up such bloody practices
And here protest eternal love to thee
And to the Queen of England specially,
Whom God hath blessed for hating papistry. 70
Navarre. These words revive my thoughts and comfort me
To see Your Highness in this virtuous mind.
Henry. Tell me, surgeon, shall I live?
Surgeon. Alas, my lord, the wound is dangerous,
For you are stricken with a poisoned knife. 75
Henry. A poisoned knife! What, shall the French King die
Wounded and poisoned both at once?
Épernon. Oh, that that damned villain were alive again,
That we might torture him with some new-found
death.
Bartas. He died a death too good. The devil of hell 80
Torture his wicked soul!
Henry. Ah, curse him not since he is dead.
Oh, the fatal poison works within my breast!
Tell me, surgeon, and flatter not: may I live?
Surgeon. Alas, my lord, Your Highness cannot live. 85
Navarre. Surgeon, why saist thou so? The King may live.
Henry. Oh no, Navarre. Thou must be King of France.
Navarre. Long may you live and still be King of France.
Épernon. Or else die, Épernon.

---

71. comfort] *Broughton (subst)*; comforts *O.*   73. SH. *Henry.*] *Dyce (subst)*; King. *O.*   74. SH. *Surgeon.*] *Ribner (subst)*; Sur. *O.*   74–5. dangerous, / For] *Broughton (subst)*; dangerous, for *O.*   76. SH. *Henry.*] *Dyce (subst)*; King. *O.*   78. SH. *Épernon.*] *Ribner (subst)*; Eper. *O.*   80. SH. *Bartas.*] *Ribner (subst)*; Bar. *O.*   80–1. hell / Torture] *Brooke (subst)*; hell torture *O.*   82. SH. *Henry.*] *Dyce (subst)*; King. *O.*   82–4. dead. / Oh ... breast! / Tell] *Broughton (subst)*; dead, *O.* ... brest, tell *O.*   82. since] *O* (sith).   85. SH. *Surgeon.*] *Ribner (subst)*; Sur. *O.*   87. SH. *Henry.*] *Dyce (subst)*; King. *O.*   89. SH. *Épernon.*] *Ribner (subst)*; Eper. *O.*

67.] i.e. that plans and implements such bloody actions as this assassination.

75. *poisoned*] Colynet describes the knife as poisoned (405).

79. *new-found death*] i.e. newly invented (and therefore most painful) manner of death.

Henry. Sweet Épernon, thy King must die. 90
My lords, fight in the quarrel of this valiant prince,
For he is your lawful king and my next heir;
Valois's line ends in my tragedy.
Now let the house of Bourbon wear the crown,
And may it never end in blood as mine hath done. 95
Weep not, sweet Navarre, but revenge my death.
Ah, Épernon, is this thy love to me?
Henry thy king wipes off these childish tears
And bids thee whet thy sword on Sixtus' bones,
That it may keenly slice the Catholics. 100
He loves me not that sheds most tears
But he that makes most lavish of his blood.
Fire Paris, where these treacherous rebels lurk.
I die, Navarre. Come, bear me to my sepulchre.

---

90. SH. *Henry.*] *Dyce (subst); King. O.* 99. Sixtus'] *Dyce 2 (subst);* Sextus *O.* 106.1. SD.] *aligned right O.*

---

91. *quarrel ... prince*] In Colynet's account, after declaring Navarre his legitimate successor, Henry charged him 'to have a special care to keep Christ's flock in unity and concord' and to 'pacify the matter of religion ... which things the King of Navarre promised to do' (407).

92.] After charging Navarre with the care of the realm, according to Colynet, Henry turned to 'the rest of [the] princes, lords and noblemen' and told them 'that the lawful succession of the royal state of France fell not to any other than to the person of Bourbon, and declared at that time the King of Navarre first successor; he prayed and exhorted the whole company to acknowledge him and to be faithful unto him' (407).

93.] 'Henry III was the last of the Valois family to rule France; they had done so for 261 years' (Esche, 404).

96.] Colynet relates that Henry 'willed him [Navarre] to make a just revenge (for example's sake) upon the authors of such a vile act' (408).

99. *Sixtus' bones*] As Esche observes, 'Pope Sixtus V died 27 August 1590; he was, therefore, alive as the King now speaks, but "remembered" as dead when the play was probably written or reported' (404).

100. *slice*] cut. '[U]sed in the sense of cut, as with a sword', the word 'is a favourite word in *Tamburlaine*' (Bennett, 252).

102. *he ... blood*] i.e. he that spills most blood (in contrast to shedding tears).

lavish] profusion, excessive abundance, extravagant outpouring or expenditure (*OED*, n.).

> Salute the Queen of England in my name, 105
> And tell her Henry dies her faithful friend.

He dies.

Navarre. Come, lords, take up the body of the King,
That we may see it honourably interred,
And then I vow for to revenge his death
As Rome and all those popish prelates there 110
Shall curse the time that e'er Navarre was King
And ruled in France by Henry's fatal death.
  They march out with the body of the King lying on
  four men's shoulders, with a dead march, drawing weapons
  on the ground.

FINIS.

112.1–2 SD.] *centred O.*

110. *As*] In such a fashion that.
112. *fatal*] 'allotted or decreed by fate or destiny; destined, fated' (*OED*, adj., 1). Oliver suggests 'fateful or (possibly) tragic' (163).
112.1–2 SD. dead march] funeral procession. The dead march involved three elements: the carrying of the corpse offstage to the sound of a drum, the trailing of soldiers' weapons, such as pikes, on the ground, and the shooting of a cannon (see *2 Tamburlaine*, 3.2.0 SD, *Hamlet*, 5.2.403, and *Coriolanus*, 5.6.149–50). Observing at least a dozen examples of this stage direction before 1603 and calling it a 'vogue term' (378) in the 1590s, Brian Cummings argues that the 'dead march' is a 'counterfeit ritual, a pastiche of religious form. Rather than an imitation of an existing practice, it appears to be an invented topos ... a rite of passage for actors and audience, a liminal theatrical space in which the boundary of the dramatic world is revealed' (379). Ironically in *The Massacre at Paris*, the fake ritual stages what 'was lost in the English Reformation' and 'act[s] out the anxieties that this loss left behind' (380).
  drawing] dragging.

APPENDIX
The Collier Leaf

[The following presents a modernised version of the Collier Leaf, based on the editor's transcription of the Folger Shakespeare Library's images of it, which are freely accessible through its website. In preparing this text, the editor consulted the transcriptions included in Oliver and Esche. The manuscript leaf provides a fuller version of the first sixteen lines of scene 19 of the play.]

Enter a Soldier *with a musket.*

Soldier. Now, sir, to you that dares make a duke a cuckold
    and use a counterfeit key to his privy chamber!
    Though you take out none but your own treasure,
    yet you put in that displeases him, and fill up his
    room that he should occupy. Herein, sir, you forestall   5
    the market and set up your standing where you
    should not. But you will say you leave him room
    enough besides. That's no answer! He's to have the
    choice of his own free land—if it be not too free,
    there's the question. Now, sir, where he is your   10
    landlord, you take upon you to be his and will needs
    enter by default. What though you were once in
    possession, yet coming upon you once unawares he
    frayed you out again. Therefore your entry is mere
    intrusion. This is against the law, sir, and though I   15
    come not to keep possession as I would I might, yet
    I come to keep you out, sir.

    1–17.] Lines 1–17 give an expanded version of the first 12 lines of scene 19. Only text unique to the Collier Leaf is glossed here.
    4. *that displeases*] i.e. that which displeases.
    12. *default*] failure to perform a task or fulfil an obligation (*OED*, n., 1a). Guise, the Soldier is suggesting, is the one who defaulted, allowing Maugiron temporarily to 'enter' and take 'possession'.
    14. *frayed*] frightened (*OED*, v.1).
    14–15. *mere intrusion*] pure trespassing.

APPENDIX

Enter Minion [MAUGIRON].

Soldier. You are welcome, sir. Have at you!

        He [Soldier] *kills him* [MAUGIRON.]

Maugiron. Traitorous Guise! Ah, thou hast murdered me!

        Enter GUISE[.]

Guise. Hold thee, tall soldier. Take thee this and fly.   20
        Exit [Soldier.]
Thus fall imperfect exhalatione,
Which our great Son of France could not effect,
A fiery meteor in the firmament.
Lie there, the King's delight and Guise's scorn.
Revenge it, Henry, if thou list or dar'st!   25
I did it only in despite of thee.
Fondly hast thou incensed the Guise's soul,
That of itself was hot enough to work
Thy just digestion with extremest shame.
The army I have gathered now shall aim   30
More at thy end than extirpation,

---

21. *exhalatione*] exhalations, vapours, meteors (*OED*, n., 3). 'So, burn the turrets of this cursèd town, / Flame to the highest region of the air', Tamburlaine proclaims as he incinerates the city in which his beloved Zenocrate died, 'And kindle heaps of exhalations / That, being fiery meteors, may presage / Death and destruction' (*2 Tamburlaine*, 3.2.1–5).

22. *Son of France*] a title reserved for the sons and grandsons of kings of France, and here referring to Henry III. 'Son' could also be 'Sun', which would continue Guise's extended astronomical metaphor: the sun (Henry) could not prevent one of its lesser lights (Maugiron) from being made to fall from its sphere of influence.

effect] have an effect upon (*OED*, v., 2), affect, alter, prevent.

23. *firmament*] heaven.

27. *Fondly*] foolishly.

incensed] enflamed.

29. *digestion*] consumption (*OED*, n., 1a).

30–3.] In scene 19 of O, Henry rather than Guise reports the information that Guise has gathered an army and explicitly raises the question of Guise's intentions: 'What your intent is yet we cannot learn, / But we presume it is not for our good' (19.19–20). O covers the same ground, then, as the Collier Leaf here in an arguably more dramatic and interesting fashion, which might suggest that the Collier Leaf represents an earlier version of the play.

31. *extirpation*] extermination of a nation, family, sect, or heresy (*OED*, n., 3a, b).

APPENDIX 139

And when thou thinkst I have forgotten this
And that thou most reposest on my faith,
Then will I wake thee from thy foolish dream
And let thee see thyself my prisoner. 35
  Exeunt [GUISE *with* MAUGIRON's *body.*]

32–5.] These lines transform the game between Guise and Henry from one of armed conflict to one of cunning and duplicity and express Guise's confidence that he will win the game against the foolish dreamer Henry. Rather than have Guise soliloquise upon the matter, scene 19 in O dramatises the onset of the game. Guise opens with a palpable lie: 'What I have done, 'tis for the Gospel's sake' (19.22). When the lie crumbles under Henry's and Épernon's concerted attack, Guise concludes in an aside that 'I must dissemble' (61) and tells Henry, 'I kiss Your Grace's hand and take my leave, / Intending to dislodge my camp with speed' (64–5). As the blinding arrogance with which he walks into his assassination two scenes later demonstrates, Guise believes that he has fooled Henry and that Henry's farewell, 'The King and thou are friends' (66), is sincere. With devastating irony, however, the rest of scene 19 and scene 21 demonstrate that it is Guise who is living a 'foolish dream'. Lulled into a false sense of security by Henry's dissembling, in lines 47–55 of scene 21 Guise gives a much more vivid version of the Caesarean fantasy he articulates in lines 22–7 of the Collier Leaf. This fantasy is immediately punctured by the following stage direction, '*Enter one of the* Murderers'. Marlowe also used this dramatic technique in *Edward II*: 'I stand as Jove's huge tree, / And others are but shrubs compared to me. / All tremble at my name, and I fear none' (25.11–13), vaunts Mortimer Junior only a few lines before the young Edward III fearlessly enters to convict him of murdering his father and command the separation of his head from his trunk. Guise displays a tragic awareness of this dramatic irony. 'Now do I but begin to look about' (53), Guise boasts before the murderer's entrance; 'Nay, then, 'tis time to look about' (68), he wryly comments after he understands what his situation really is.

Index

advertised 20.1
agent 24.50
d'Albret, Jeanne 3, 55, 56, 62
Allott, Robert 57
Alençon, François Duke of 3, 7, 8, 9, 28, 92, 96, 121, 125
amain 20.17
an 4.40, 21.116
animated 19.44
anon 21.11
argent 5.2
array 15.16
as 24.110
attendance 2.48

becomes 11.14
bent 14.20, 21.1
bewray 21.150
blockish 9.50
Bodin, Jean 31, 32
de Bourbon-Condé, Henry 3, 6, 9, 51, 53, 77, 92, 100, 107
bowels 2.77
brainpan 3.19
broil 9.72
brook 19.58
brother 1.1
brunt 16.16
burgonets 4.30
but 16.8

cabinet 21.27
Caesar 2, 61, 90, 118, 119, 120, 129
Cardinal of Guise, Louis 8, 10, 15, 20, 23, 24, 37, 54, 58, 73, 88, 93, 121
Caruth, Cathy 18, 26
cast 24.16
cause 19.26
challenge 4.8
de Chambes, Jean, Count of Montsoreau 21, 74, 76
changeling 21.141

Charles IX 3, 4, 14, 19, 23, 51, 52, 58, 66
Clément, Jacques 1, 11, 127, 128, 130
close 21.13
closely 5.58
de Clèves, Catherine 97
de Coligny, Gaspard, Seigneur de Châtillon 3, 4, 5, 6, 12, 17, 19, 20, 21, 39, 41, 42, 51, 53, 55, 56, 62, 65, 68, 69, 70, 71, 72, 73, 74, 77, 78, 86, 87, 88
colleges 2.79
collier 9.55
Collier Leaf 46, 137–9
colours 16.22
common 2.39
complices 20.11
comprised 2.85
consummate 1.19
Council of Trent 111
counterfeit 19.2
countermand 19.42, 21.136
counterpoise 2.57
Coutras, Battle of 8, 9, 97, 100, 101, 103, 106, 112
covenant 10.21
cràsed 24.63
cross 1.16
crowns 2.31
cuckold 19.1

darts 9.61
daughter 1.14
Day of Barricades 9, 10, 107, 114
declaim 9.53
decreed 4.4
defend 16.8
deserts 10.3
disgorge 21.22
disgrace 17.22, 17.24
dislodge 19.65
dispensation 2.62

disports 14.41
Douai 26, 121
drawing 24.112.2 SD
drench 22.10
durst 4.55

Edict of Nantes 8, 22, 30
effecting 19.73
Elizabeth I 7, 26, 27, 28, 32, 35, 42, 107, 120, 121, 131, 132
else 2.48, 19.40
entrance 5.12
envious 1.29
entombs 2.76
epitomes 9.29
ere 20.13
exclaim 21.142
excommunication 120, 121, 128
exhibition 19.38

faith 17.15
fatal 4.2, 24.112
file 22.3
fire 24.62
follow 2.95
forestall 19.4
forsooth 9.31
framed 2.64
fruit 15.31
fuelled 1.8

gear 19.11
gentle 4.13
girting 24.14
Globe theatre 39, 77
Golding, Arthur 12, 22, 58
Gondi, Albert, Count of Retz 65, 70, 76
de Gonzague Louis 65, 70, 73, 76
Goulart, Simon 12, 17, 77
guerdon 2.11
Guise, François Duke of 3, 53, 56
Guise, Henry Duke of 4, 5, 6, 8, 9, 10, 11, 12, 13, 14, 15, 16, 17, 19, 20, 21, 22, 23, 24, 25, 26, 37, 38, 40, 41, 53, 54, 55, 56, 58–9, 60, 61, 62, 63, 65, 66, 67, 68, 69, 70, 71, 72, 73, 74, 75, 76, 77, 78, 82, 83, 87, 88, 89, 93, 94, 96, 97, 100, 103, 107, 109, 110, 112, 114, 121, 122

haughty 16.21
Henry III (Anjou) 1, 3, 4, 7, 8, 9, 10, 11, 12, 14, 17, 19, 21, 23, 24, 25, 26, 27, 28, 32, 34, 36, 37, 38, 39, 59, 65, 66, 68, 70, 71, 84, 92, 93, 103, 120, 134, 138
Henry IV (Navarre) 2, 3, 4, 5, 6, 7, 8, 9, 11, 14, 15, 16, 18, 19, 20, 23, 25, 27, 36, 37, 38, 51, 54, 59, 65, 75, 77, 82, 83, 88, 89, 90, 92, 96, 100, 101, 103, 106, 108, 112, 113, 131, 134
Henslowe, Philip 39, 40, 44, 45, 86
hold 3.2, 19.11
Holy League 9, 10, 11, 13, 16, 24, 36, 96, 103, 109
Hotman, François 7, 12, 13, 17, 20, 23, 51, 53, 55, 56, 62, 63, 65, 66, 67, 68, 69, 70, 72, 73, 74, 75, 76, 77, 81, 83, 84, 86, 87, 88

imperious 17.17
import 2.53
incensed 16.14, 24.63
inventions 16.8

de Joyeuse, Anne 9, 91, 100, 102, 103, 106
juror 19.33

keep 2.83, 5.16

LaCapra, Dominick 18, 22
largesse 2.61
latter 9.41
lavish 24.102
leaves 10.23
Lee, Nathaniel 19
levelled 2.36
de Lévis, Gabriel, Seigneur de Léran 15, 21, 75
lie 24.13
list 19.15
de Louviers, Charles, Seigneur de Maurevet 5, 56

lowered 2.1
lusty 11.13
Lutetia 24.13

Machiavellianism 2, 15, 16, 37, 38, 60
made 9.74
makes 2.23
manage 10.9
Marlowe, Christopher 1–2
  Dido Queen of Carthage 2, 45
  Doctor Faustus 2, 39, 40, 58, 75, 101
  Edward II 2, 14, 19, 45, 100, 110, 111, 113, 139
  The Jew of Malta 2, 29, 39, 45, 60, 125, 126
  1 Tamburlaine 2, 20, 21, 23, 39, 45
  2 Tamburlaine 2, 21, 23, 29, 34–6, 39, 45, 85, 126, 134, 135, 137
marry 17.34
martial 10.5
massacre 4.58
Massacre at Paris 2–8
  assassinations of the Queen of Navarre and the Admiral 5–6
  death toll 6
  international response 7
  royal council 6
  spread to provinces 6
  wedding of Navarre and Margaret Valois 2–5
matins 9.86
de Maugiron, Louis 8, 25, 94, 97
Mayenne, Charles Duke of 11, 12, 54, 93, 94, 107, 126
meaning 19.63
meddle 3.14
de Medici, Catherine 1, 3, 4, 6, 7, 8, 17, 21, 23, 34, 36, 37, 38, 52, 54, 65, 68, 87, 88, 89, 125
minions 14.03. SD
miscreant 21.142
misdo 13.11
mocks 17.20
de Mornay, Philippe, Seigneur de Plessis Marly 90, 92

Mount Faucon 73, 86
moved 19.28
mounted 21.27

native 1.6
near 5.37
need 17.15
nephew 4.24
noted 4.5

occupy 19.7
offencious 9.23
once 1.36
Ottoman Empire 29, 32, 33, 34, 35, 36, 61, 84, 85
oubliance 22, 23

papacy 3, 7, 8, 9, 23, 26, 37, 38, 54, 59, 73, 100, 103, 107, 109, 110, 114, 119, 120, 121, 124, 125, 132
partial 5.51
parts 24.42
paws 22.10
pedants 9.65
pension 2.62
perform 2.30
perfume 3.4
persist 14.21
physic 21.87
pit 21.32
places 9.44
plaints 12.5
plant 14.49
pleasantness 14.44
Poland 29, 32, 34, 84, 85, 86, 91, 92, 93, 94
policy 2.64
poniard 9.79
popelings 20.25
post 20.8
power 16.15
prejudice 10.17
present 4.66, 19.75
prevented 23.13
prithee 15.14
progeny 1.8
prop 23.4
proper 4.14
prove 1.11

quiddity 9.33

de la Ramée, Pierre 37, 77, 78, 79, 80
reduced 9.46
Reims 1, 26, 93, 95, 121
relents 4.9
removeless 14.22
rent 16.6
requite 2.20
respect 16.23
resteth 13.19
Rose theatre 39–40, 43, 68, 77, 83, 86
Rothberg, Michael 18
ruth 18.11

de Salluste, Guillaume, Seigneur du Bartas 101
scourge 13.9
seat 2.103
seem 13.39
seen 9.29
senate 14.6
Serres, Jean 12, 89, 123, 125, 130
sectious 19.46
see 20.26
Shakespeare, William 14, 18, 45, 57, 118
simple 19.63
sirrah 7.1
slack 14.20
slice 24.100
smack 9.24
sort 21.97
sound 9.25
Spain 3, 4, 7, 8, 9, 23, 26, 56, 59, 61, 92, 100, 101, 109, 110, 120, 121
Spanish Armada 26, 121
speed 14.14
standard-bearer 5.11
standing 19.5, 21.10
state 14.7
stately 2.57
stay 1.23, 9.72, 13.1, 21.75, 23.5
steal 13.32
stoop 21.138

store 2.31
storm 1.27, 11.44
straggling 4.2
straight 2.24
strange 16.8
strumpet 15.34, 24.14
subscribe 19.78
suffer 17.5
supply 3.27
surcease 18.6
surcharged 21.23
surfeiting 24.15

tall 19.13
Talon, Omer 37, 78
therfore 1637
timeless 1.45
toil 1.53
toleration 7, 29–39
train 21.37
tragical 19.88
trap 1.52
trauma 16–29, 44
traumatic realism 18
trothless 15.23
tyranny 17, 90, 128

unjust 15.23

de la Valette, Jean-Louis, Duke of Épernon 38, 41, 91
de Valois, Marguerite 2, 3, 4, 19, 20, 51, 52, 54, 59, 75, 97
vaunt 16.25
vouchsafed 24.8

wait 2.48
wanton 21.51
wants 4.32
wars of religion 3, 7, 8, 9, 22, 29, 30, 31, 53, 87, 92, 100, 121
watchword 4.36
wherefore 9.6
will 9.82, 21.125
would 19.10, 21.140
wrack 19.54, 21.154

yoked 21.111

EU authorised representative for GPSR:
Easy Access System Europe, Mustamäe tee 50,
10621 Tallinn, Estonia
gpsr.requests@easproject.com

www.ingramcontent.com/pod-product-compliance
Ingram Content Group UK Ltd.
Pitfield, Milton Keynes, MK11 3LW, UK
UKHW021841140426
5217IPUK00022B/1542